Earning Freemasonry

A One Day Class Redemption

———————

Adam T. Osman, Past Master

Earning Freemasonry – A One Day Class Redemption

ISBN-13:
978-1494981457

ISBN-10:
1494981459

Printed in the United States of America

This book is dedicated to Freemasons who have lost their way and those who were sent down the wrong path to begin with.

Pictured above: Thomas H. Osman, P.M. and Adam T. Osman, P.M.
with the George Washington Gavel in 2012

About the Author

Adam T. Osman is a member and Past Master of Juniata Lodge No. 282 in Hollidaysburg, PA. In 2011 he was awarded the Grand Lodge of Pennsylvania's Proficiency Award for being proficient in all three symbolic degrees. In 2013 he became a certified Master Masonic Scholar by the Grand Lodge of Pennsylvania's Academy of Masonic Knowledge.

He is also a 32nd degree Mason in the Valley of Altoona of the Ancient Accepted Scottish Rite, Northern Masonic Jurisdiction. He is a member of the Jaffa Shrine (Mid-Atlantic Shrine Association) of the Shriners International where he holds membership in the Jaffa Shrine Provost Guard Unit as well as the Jaffa Shrine Hillbilly Clan No. 74. In 2013 he was one of three winners in the 2nd Annual Shriners International Personal Essay Contest. He is also a member of Bedford Chapter No. 255 of the Grand Holy Royal Arch Chapter of PA.

Adam is a 2005 graduate of Indiana University of Pennsylvania with a bachelor's degree in Communications Media. While at IUP he was a member of the Gamma Pi Chapter of the Delta Sigma Phi fraternity where he served many offices including chaplain, pledge education chair, and secretary. He currently lives in Alum Bank Pa with his beautiful wife Traci and three children, Owen, Lillian, and Robin.

Acknowledgements

I want to thank my father and Past Master Thomas H. Osman for helping me with all things Masonic and teaching me to never go through the motions if the job is not going to get done. To my Lodge and all my brethren for their support and motivation, I could not have become a better person without you all. Also, I am grateful for the Pennsylvania Academy of Masonic Knowledge and the coursework, meetings, and presentations they provided. This program was by far the most influential part of my Masonic development. To Bro. Shawn Gorley for the motivation in showing me that a book will not just write itself. I am also thankful for the online world of Masonic brethren, podcasts, blogs, research resources, and social media. These guys hundreds of miles away have been just as helpful as brothers next door. To Bro. Bobby Snyder, DDGM (PA34) and Bro. Dale De Lozier, PDDGM (PA20) for their Masonic knowledge and leadership. Also, I need to thank my friends Dan Klyne and Randy Smith for their grammatical proofreading. Someday I hope to sit with you both in Lodge. I also want to say thank you to Faith Hoenstine who changed my life forever by sending me on my path in Freemasonry. Last but not least to my wife and entire family for putting up with my meetings and Masonic exploration. I acknowledge your tolerance for my habit and addiction to Freemasonry.

Preface

There are many reasons why an average Joe will look to the Masonic fraternity for membership. It isn't often talked about, but many times men look to the fraternity for all the wrong reasons. Whether or not we want to admit it, some of the best men and the most dedicated Masons of today have begun their Masonic journey under misguided information.

When asking around any Lodge for reasons men chose to seek membership in Freemasonry one will probably find varying reasons like; "I wanted to become a better person." to "I wanted to be a part of a noble and benevolent society." While these reasons are great, generally you hear these statements AFTER these men become members.

Unfortunately, the sad reality for many people is that the above statements are not the actual reason they sought membership.

In reality, what many men won't say out loud after they join is that the real reasons were somewhere between the lines of; "My dad was a Mason," to "I want to get out of speeding tickets," to "I thought I'd advance in my job being a Mason." In other words, many men, even the ones that rise to be great Freemasons, do not originally join for the right reasons.

We should know as Masons that the above reasons, if verbally communicated, are absolutely red flags that should end a candidate's interview. However, this rarely happens. It has even been practice by some interviewing Masons to explain what Masonry IS and IS NOT before the petitioner says a word in the interview. When this is done, low and behold, a man who wanted to join with the intention of getting out of a speeding ticket suddenly wants to just be a better man.

In a perfect world, statements like the above, if said during an interview, should end the process and advancement of the petitioner at that very moment. In a perfect world the petitioner being interviewed should never even have gotten that far with any thoughts or false notion of social, personal, or financial gain.

In a perfect world the system would weed out the under qualified and misinformed men leaving nothing but well and duly prepared men ready to take the oaths of Freemasonry. In reality, however, the system isn't perfect.

There are many reasons misinformed men slip past the interviewing committee. Sadly, in today's fraternity, sometimes the interviewers may be just as misguided as the petitioner. Other times the interviewers may let such statements slide because they themselves also thought the same before taking their degrees.

Whatever the reasons for the relaxation of the order, this book aims to aid in the restoration of the fraternity by helping members earn Freemasonry. It is this author's opinion and personal experience that restoration starts with becoming informed as a Mason. With the ever easing process of becoming a Mason it is more important now than ever to earn Freemasonry.

Because this book is written largely from personal experience, I don't expect anyone to agree with me 100%. Freemasonry is a journey to self-betterment. Since everyone can interpret things slightly differently in their own journey, you may find yourself disagreeing with the way I see things or the suggestions I make. I'm ok with that.

Why Write this Book?

I was inspired to write this book in part due to the shortcuts which were thrown at me in my own Masonic journey, but more especially to highlight the need for all Masons to earn Freemasonry and redeem their membership for its true purpose. While it is my opinion that the one day class Mason generally has a bit more catch up to do, it's important for all Masons, regardless of how they were made, to be familiar with the true intention and practices of the Craft if they want to get the most out of their membership.

As I will explain in the following paragraphs, I want you to keep in mind that I simply went along with the way things were. As an uninformed non-Mason I had very little idea that what I doing was not the typical way things were traditionally done. As I quickly found out, these "shortcuts" became not only massive hurdles, but also a constant black mark that has bothered me my entire Masonic career.

The more I became involved, the more I realized that if I wanted to stand out and prove myself as a Freemason I would have to do a little more than just work my way through the chairs. I set the goal of doing whatever I had to do to earn Freemasonry. I did not want to do this just for the sake of gaining the respect of the brethren who disagree with the new Masonic short cuts that seem to be popping up everywhere, but for myself, to gain back what I had been deprived of by taking so many shortcuts.

I think it is important to state upfront this is not going to be about learning Freemasonry. Any half-motivated man can learn what Freemasonry is supposed to be about. This will be about earning Freemasonry. It is my hope that this book will help you understand and put to use the teachings and working tools of Freemasonry so that you can pay it forward to the next misguided brother.

To say that we have a couple guys in our ranks that have been misled or are misleading is an understatement. Some men rush to memorize 10,000 words of the ritual and become Worshipful Master, but never take the time to really think about what exactly the ritual is teaching.

We've all seen the monotone robotic recital of a degree. We have also seen the Speedy Gonzales dash to the finish line degree recital. While they may be word for word spot on accurate, many times that is ALL they are.

While learning the ritual and floor work is part of our duty as Freemasons and Lodge leaders, it's what we do with the knowledge after we get it that counts.

Observing the above and correcting my own course in Freemasonry gave me the desire to fulfill my obligation as a Mason. By attempting to reach other men who may have drifted off course, or, in some cases, never left the dock to begin with, this is an attempt to address our failings and shortcomings as a whole the best way I know how, with storytelling and tough love.

Through Masonic education, reading books, and learning how to use the working tools I firmly believe that I have earned Freemasonry, despite all the short cuts I originally took.

Through dedication, trial, and lots of error, eventually I became proficient in the degree work, was elected Worshipful Master, and became a certified Master Masonic Scholar through the

Grand Lodge of Pennsylvania's Academy of Masonic Knowledge. Even with any achievement I have under my belt I still continue my work at personal refinement.

I do not now, nor do I ever foresee a time in the future when I will claim or think I am any sort of Masonic Master Authority. While titles are on occasion bestowed upon the individual for achievement, we need to look no further than our working tool, the level, which teaches us that we all have the exact same opportunities in Freemasonry. My exact experience and achievements are available for you if you chose to seek it for yourself.

The One Day Class

One day classes used to be a rare occurrence, but not completely unheard of. Other Jurisdictions had been doing them for a few years. While it may seem to some that a one day class is completely unacceptable and inefficient, it is worth pointing out that many Grand Lodges have practices and resources in place for any new Mason, be he a one day class Mason or traditional, to help them adjust to Masonry and find everything they need as new members. For many, however, much of these resources are lost to men who never come back to Lodge or do not care enough about what they just saw to lean more. The resources available, while for the new member, also rely heavily on post-one day class promotion by the Lodges and existing brethren.

A new member is typically told at his first meeting about everything they need to know to get "caught up to speed" on what they missed. Where I think the ball gets dropped sometimes is that simply stating to a Lodge of new and unfamiliar members what is available, many times, simply isn't enough when dealing with timid or unfamiliar new men.

On one hand the argument can be made that you can lead a horse to water but you can't make him drink. By this, I mean, you, as a secretary, Worshipful Master, or a Lodge, can tell the members what they need and should do, but if the member doesn't take it upon himself to actually do it, then it's his loss. After all, you told him. You did your job. This is a strong argument, as anyone knows that you typically cannot help a person who will not help himself.

Going back to the "You can lead a horse to water but you can't make him drink." cliché, on the other hand, you as secretary, Worshipful Master, or Lodge can't just point to the top of the mountain and say, "The water bucket is up there, it's all yours, go get it." and expect anything to happen. As much as the horse may want a drink of water, simply stating one or two times where to go may not be effective.

While some Lodges and districts, I am sure, have mandatory education and mentoring, sadly many do not, or at least are not implemented efficiently enough to be as successful as they could, or should, have been.

Many one day classes take a massive coordinated effort by several Lodges throughout the district, or, as in my case, the coordinated effort of many districts throughout the region. The District Deputy Grand Masters and Worshipful Masters of the Lodges have to be involved and supportive to make them successful.

It's important to understand that your Grand Master is the absolute authority in your Jurisdiction and when he says there will be a one day class, regardless if you 100% in agreement with it or not, you have a general obligation to help out to the best of your ability and make the most of it.

My district, PA D20, had an overwhelmingly successful one day class. According to the November Pennsylvania Freemason Magazine, over 4000 men were made Masons on October 02, 2004. District 20 was one of the top 5 districts for new members in 2004. I would argue that it was planned and executed the best way it possibly could have been by the best team of men who could have planned it.

Since 2004 my district, in particular my Lodge, has had no shortage of dedicated one day class men fulfilling their obligations as Freemasons and Lodge officers. From 2004-2014 Juniata Lodge No. 282 has had three Worshipful Masters that were products of the 2004 or 2005 one day classes in Pennsylvania. While there are success stories, there are far too many situations where our follow up and mentoring fell short.

While the leaders in charge of these efforts get behind them and make the core purpose of the one day class programs successful, I feel the underlying and post one day class efforts fall short many times.

Section One:

A Path to Freemasonry

Planting the Seed

For me, the desire to become a Freemason, believe it or not, originally came from an appendant Masonic body. Ironically, the organization that opened my eyes to Freemasonry has also been one that I find myself criticizing from time to time for steering people away from Freemasonry. Strangely, the person I credit for changing my life and leading me to Freemasonry was a girl with a very serious illness.

When I was in tenth grade, like any 16-year-old, I did not think about things like health insurance or medical care. I had never been faced with serious illness or had to witness hardship brought on by a hospital stay. Up until this point in my life everyone I knew seemed to have been healthy other than the occasional cold or broken bone. It was this year that I first saw true hardship close to home. It was at this time that a girl who went to my school, whom I did not know, contracted spinal meningitis.

At first I didn't pay much attention to the teachers talking about it, or give much thought to how serious it was. Then I remember the matter evolving into a very big deal. Before too long there were fundraisers being held and communities donating assistance to this girl and her family.

Things seemed to keep going from bad to worse. Within a few months she had lost several body parts from the illness. All hope seemed lost and I remember on more than one occasion hearing about how they had to make another amputation. I remember hearing on more than one occasion that she was probably going to die. This is when the Shriners got involved.

Like many people, I went to the Shrine Circus when I was young. I could recognize a Shriner by his funny red hat and I enjoyed watching the big guys with the tiny cars in the parades. Outside of that I had no clue what the true missions of the Shriners were. It was then, for the first time in my life, when I learned who the Shriners were and what they did for the community.

I started to hear the word Shriner more and more, and it typically wasn't accompanied by the phrases "funny red hat" or "circus."

While I am sure it would be unfair to credit JUST the Shriners for saving this girls life, what sticks out in my head is the constant stories of them transporting her, caring for her, getting her whatever she needed, and doing it all free of charge to the family.

For the next few years I learned more and more about the Shriners and their mission. I learned about burn units and pediatric research centers. Suddenly these guys with the funny hats and tiny cars actually meant something to me. I was captivated by an organization of men who brought so much joy to families and communities.

As I moved through high school I was fortunate enough to meet a few Shriners, including my oldest cousin, who told me about the process of becoming a Shriner. These men led me to research Freemasonry where I gained a great amount of respect for not just one fraternity of men that were helping children, but a whole society of men with upright morals and rectitude of conduct.

I learned of a society of men who were all equal - on the level so to speak - despite what church they belonged to, where they worked, or how much money they made. I found a complete fraternity of men that used symbols like the plumb, level, and square to teach life morals of citizenship, acceptance, honor, and virtue.

I knew, without a doubt, that I wanted to someday be a part of this large and noble organization of men. I could not wait to become of age and take upon myself the oaths and obligations which I continue live by every day of my life.

Starting the Journey

My first inquiries into Freemasonry happened shortly after I turned 18 in December of 2000. At that time in Pennsylvania, a man had to be 21 years old before petitioning the Lodge. I was let down, but looked forward to December 2003 when I could ask again. Little did I know that in March of 2002 the Grand Lodge of Pennsylvania amended the *Digest of Decisions* by lowering "mature age" to 18 and I could have sought membership at that time if I had known. Regardless, by early 2004 I was seeking membership again.

After inquiring, it was brought to my attention that if I wanted to "hold off" until October that I could become a Freemason in one day as opposed to the traditional three month period that it normally takes. Being uninformed and away at college, this option seemed to make perfect sense to me. I had no reason to think this wasn't the typical way things worked.

Unknown to me at the time, because of the one day class membership grab, there were many people who were also "holding off" becoming Masons. Because this was a unique situation and the one day classes a fairly new concept, many times special dispensations, small changes in interviewing, and some liberties had to be taken to meet the demands of interviewing large numbers of men and coordinating an event of this caliber.

For this reason, I, along with my father and brother, was summoned to the Lodge with a number of other people to have my interview conducted.

I did not find out until later that this was not the traditionally accepted method of having an interview conducted, but again, this was not a traditional overall event. Regardless, the men I met, and the man who conducted my interview were friendly, informative, and very helpful. It was here when I learned about other membership opportunities that were taking place the exact same day as the one day class.

I had no idea that the interviews were to be conducted at the petitioner's house. At this point everything still seemed to me as through I was doing exactly what others who had come before me had done.

I became a member of Juniata Lodge No. 282 in Hollidaysburg, Pennsylvania on October 02, 2004. I was part of the "One Day Man to Mason Journey" which was authorized by the Jurisdiction of the Grand Lodge of Pennsylvania.

While I did know that the one day classes weren't typical at this point, it never dawned on me why. For me, it seemed like a great opportunity to get things out of the way and get started with my membership in this "secret society" as I incorrectly looked at it.

When I became a Mason I was not in a Lodge room, but rather in the auditorium of the Jaffa Shrine in Altoona, Pennsylvania. I was not alone being led by my friend and guide either, but rather, sitting on a metal folding chair shoulder to shoulder with over 400 men.

Despite my best intentions and expectations of the day, I sat near the back, took in almost nothing, and found that for much of the three degrees I was distracted, confused, disinterested, and simply found myself just playing along in order to get to the end of the day. I tried to focus and watch the degree work, but found myself constantly distracted by other things in the room.

I'm not saying my attention and actions were appropriate, but I had no idea what I was supposed to be experiencing, and so I had no idea what I was missing out on.

As the degrees concluded and we got a few minute break before the next degree took place I remember hearing phrases like "brought to light" and "due guard" but I couldn't tell you at all what this stuff meant, let alone remember experiencing it.

Shortly after the third degree finished we had lunch then headed back to the auditorium for the Scottish Rite degrees. That day I witnessed a few degrees including the 32nd degree of the Scottish Rite Northern Jurisdiction. These degrees were, of course, different than the Blue Lodge degrees, but since I had little clue what was going on, and the same distractions of 400 still around me, I didn't take in much of them either.

Another short break happened and we returned once again to the auditorium where I was made a member of Ancient Arabic Order of the Nobles of the Mystic Shrine, The Shriners.

At the end of the day I drove back to college with pretty much no retention of what I had just been through. I had a cool fez, a bunch of paperwork on appendant and concordant Masonic bodies, and the right to call myself a 32nd degree Mason. Keep in mind this was all in one day. Other than my interview, which incorrectly took place at the Lodge, this was my only Masonic experience to date.

Road Blocks in Short Cuts

As uninformed as I was, I still felt like jumping right in and learning more. My first actual Lodge meeting was an intimidating experience. I knew very few people, had no clue what I was supposed to be doing, and to make it worse, when I walked in with my father and brother we sat on the opposite side of the Lodge that was the accepted normal side. It wasn't technically wrong to sit on that side, but no one said a word to us or pointed out that, for whatever reason, it was tradition to sit in the north. (Others may note here that in some Lodges it is traditional that everyone sits in the south. Other Lodges are a nice even split on both sides.)

It was a very awkward situation sitting in the meeting with an entire Lodge of men staring back at us. Because of this we couldn't even hide the fact that we didn't properly know how to throw the signs or know when to stand up or sit down. This was just the first of many awkward or embarrassing situations I accredit in part to my short cut to Master Mason.

Another thing that slapped me in the face with all my new memberships was the reality of commitment and paying dues. Sure, in less than 12 hours I became a member of three separate fraternities, but when I started to step back and figure out a few things I realized that maybe I should have done a little more research before committing to so many organizations.

As a new member, I looked at all Masonic bodies much the way my wife still looks at them. That is, when I went out the door to a meeting, no matter what meeting, I viewed it as going to "the Masons."

I had a general assumption that these organizations were full of the same guys who all knew each other and worked in harmony and each body loved, promoted, respected, and supported each other.

The more I tried to get involved in one body, the more I became confused as to why the other bodies do things differently. I met Masons who were old school and upset about the one day classes. I met Shriners who hadn't been to a Lodge meeting in thirty years. I met other Masons who were downright removed from everything Masonic.

Also, joining in October, it wasn't very long until dues notices started pouring in and adding up. Originally I had $50 for Blue Lodge, $75 for Shrine, and I believe it was $65 for Scottish Rite. Trying to keep up with all the meetings was one thing, but coming up with 190 dollars right away was a little intimidating as well.

Still, I knew it was part of the game and I was still proud to call myself a Freemason. At first I tried to keep up with the meetings. I was an hour and a half away at college, but I tried to do the stated, extra, rehearsal, and school of instruction for Blue Lodge. I tied to go to Consistory once a month for Scottish Rite. I even found a Shrine club in my college town that would give me a connection to the Shrine without having to drive an hour and a half to stay informed. The Shrine club was convenient, and all for the low dues cost of another fifteen dollars a year.

All of the meetings, dues, and running combined with the realization after a couple months that I wasn't in a secret society at all, but rather three separate fraternities and a Shrine club and I knew nothing about any of them.

Where was all of the mystery and symbols? Where were the secret handshakes that these guys were supposed to be using among each other? Where was the brotherhood and personal benefit?

I was not only confused, I found myself just about broke, tired of wasting my time driving to meetings that sometimes had no program, and eventually became slightly resentful.

It eventually became clear to me that I was not ready, qualified, or desirous to be in so many bodies, despite constant other bodies and clubs seeking membership from me. I made the decision to cut back.

While I still had over 200 dollars in dues each year, which is only a small fraction of what many other men pay, I cut back to stated meetings, and Shrine club meetings.

Eventually I graduated college and moved closer to my Masonic geographic area. I resigned membership from my Shrine club since I wasn't about to be driving back to college once a month to be informed about the Shrine I now lived close to, and I did my best to budget my dues so it wasn't a shock each year when the notices came.

Overall I felt a little cheated. With all of the best intentions for gaining membership and exposing Freemasonry to more people, I felt the system as a whole set me up to trap me. I felt let down. For everyone who told me about how Freemasonry is going to make me a better person, I hardly felt like I was fitting into that category.

Learning Freemasonry

Given no real guidance, but getting to know a few more people, I eventually settled into a groove and started to learn the way things went. I focused on Blue Lodge, went to meetings, paid my dues, and started to learn some of the floor work.

While it had become clear to me that the shortcuts I took were nothing more than road blocks, I eventually got to the point where I knew what being brought to light meant, even though I never had the chance to experience it personally. I could recognize all of the signs and due guards. I even learned all the handshakes, even though hardly anyone used them.

I learned quite a bit about Freemasonry and the ritual, but still, I just didn't get why this was supposed to be some life altering society of self-betterment. I was in the chair line and from year to year advanced and learned a little more, but I hardly felt like my life was being made any better.

I found that no one really pushed education, and more often than not the programs had very little to do with Freemasonry. We'd show up and pay bills and listen to the secretary, but when it was all said and done, there just wasn't very much more to it.

I had been given the tools of Freemasonry, but not the instruction on how to use them. I started to equate my Masonic experience with that of a child who has been handed ownership of the family business, even though I didn't build or earn it. The gears kept moving, the system kept running, but I still had little notion as to what supposedly made us such a large and noble society.

The further I got in Freemasonry, the more I realized that simply learning the floor work and ritual of the Craft was not going to make me a better person. While I love all of my Lodge brethren, and I value their friendship and fellowship, I knew that if I wanted to take my Masonic membership to the next level I was going to have to take it upon myself to do so.

Over the years I felt as though I eventually learned what I had missed. I rarely missed a stated meeting and hardly ever sat on the side lines. I was no super Mason by any means and I still have more flaws than a lot of Masons. I reached a point where I knew that I was going to have to move from simply learning Freemasonry to earning Freemasonry.

Earning Freemasonry

When I became a Mason I was very proud, but the more involved I became, the more I realized that I had been shown a lot of shortcuts. On a path to earning my keep in the Lodge I found that these shortcuts were largely nothing more than extra hurdles that I had to clear in order to feel like a proven and contributing member. While any Mason, be it one day class or traditional, is every bit a "member in good standing" and "entitled to all the rights and privileges of the Lodge" he can't expect to automatically just know everything right away. In one sense, he is entitled to the privileges the same way I am entitled to a pay check after I am hired for a job. I have to work hard first in order to get it.

As I worked my way through the chairs to become Worshipful Master in 2012 I knew there would be a lot of pressure to perform. While trying to be viewed as a leader to the new members, I felt it was necessary to show the older traditional members that I knew what I was doing.

I took my oath to lead the Lodge very seriously and for that entire year I did everything in my power to keep things in order. Despite a few disagreements here and there, I found myself with an extremely helpful line up of officers. I credit much of my positive highlights in my year as Worshipful Master to all of my elected and appointed officers.

This year we had an overwhelmingly successful year for fundraising as well as a Masonic education program every month. Although we had an extremely successful year, I found myself wanting to do more.

During my time as Master I enrolled in the Pennsylvania Academy of Masonic Knowledge. This program was designed to increase your Masonic knowledge and improve you as a Mason. In the words of their own mission statement:

"The Pennsylvania Academy of Masonic Knowledge will strive to create an environment that will encourage Masons to seek a greater understanding of the nature and purposes of Freemasonry in all its many aspects-past, present, and future-and to share that understanding with others.

To this end, the Academy will offer learning opportunities in which Masons may participate in dialogues with similarly inclined brethren, witness prominent Masonic scholars discussing various aspects of Freemasonry, and pursue home study at their own pace and in their own areas of interest, through publications on Masonic subjects recommended by the Academy.

In addition to providing a learning experience for Freemasons, the Academy will be a vehicle affording recognition to Masons who share their knowledge of Freemasonry with fellow Masons or the public by the written or spoken word."

In one aspect, this program is essentially what every single Mason SHOULD be doing in Lodge each month simply because he is a Freemason in my opinion.

It was truly an eye opener for me in helping me understand Freemasonry inside and out by learning deeper esoteric Masonic history, philosophy, and ritual. The program is set up in three levels. It can be done at your own pace and much of the grading is more verification that you understood what the topic was.

While I never set out to rush through this course, as I learned the hard way early in my Masonic career to pace myself, in reality once the door to esoteric Freemasonry had been opened for me I found myself engrossed in reading book after book, which aided in my program creation and Masonic discussions.

Because I had already been doing Masonic programs and presentations at my Lodge long before I knew the Academy existed I was able to back date a few of my presentations for credit toward my certification level.

Because of the backdated credits, I fulfilled my requirements to be certified as a Master Masonic Scholar by April 2013. I feel I have earned Freemasonry. I finally feel that I have earned back what I had missed, and what was not given me.

The more I benefit from Freemasonry, the more I see others missing out the same way I did. There are many good men falling by the wayside every day and I felt like it was my obligation to give back and help spread the light. I started blogging a few years ago on subject matters that I had an opinion on. I ask no one to agree with me, but I would feel like I was cheating my brethren if I at least didn't try to share my struggle to earn Freemasonry. While my hope is that my stories and suggestions can help the entire fraternity, I would be happy to know my experience help even a single brother.

To be honest with you, this was never intended to be a book. When I started out writing a blog post with suggestions to new members how to earn Freemasonry, it quickly became apparent to me that telling new members where to turn to find answers will only work if those places actually had the answers. What I realized is that many of the so called resources out there were full of people who could use a little education of their own. Our fraternity is a complicated system of men of all levels of rank and title. From the new member, to the card carrier, to the regular attendees, officers, and even Past Masters, there is no shortage of men who seemingly have been slipping by without ever actually earning Freemasonry.

We have men who have been given all the tools, have been told all the secrets, shown all the handshakes, listened to all of the rituals and have been exposed to all of our knocks, passwords, floor work and resources, but still many of these men treat the order as though it's a regular golf club or civic organization. To

this, I say, if all you are looking for in a group is a little social connection and civic action from time to time, Freemasonry should not have been your first choice.

In light of this, you are either here now, or you want to learn a little more about Freemasonry, and as long as you are a good person and continue to pay your dues, you will most likely be here tomorrow. If you truly want to call yourself a Freemason, I firmly believe it is time for all of us to earn what we have been given.

This book is meant to help you uncover which type of Mason you are. It is possible that you may not even know yourself. If all you have ever learned about Masonry has been passed to you from equally uniformed Masons, you may never have actually experienced the true beauty and benefits of the Craft.

In your degree work you were symbolically brought to Masonic light unless you were like me and were raised in a one day class, in which case you were not symbolically brought to Masonic light and arguably were not even symbolically "raised."

In true Freemasonry, you put the symbolism to work as you find the light of Freemasonry. When it happens, you will know it. It's like a light bulb that just clicks on. It doesn't just happen though. It takes a little bit of effort on your part. While trying not to be too cliché; some say you get out of it what you put into it. This is true, but as a dedicated Mason, it is this author's firm belief that you will get 10 times more back than what you put into.

Another reason to write this book is based on what I mentioned above. I am a product of a one day class. There is much debate on the effectiveness of such classes. I am not about to make this book a vilification of one day Masons, or Jurisdictions that sponsor and support one day Masons. That doesn't mean I don't have an opinion on such things, and, as a way to earn Freemasonry, I feel it would be inappropriate and less than helpful if I did not point out a few of my first hand observations.

As far as one day classed go overall, my opinion is that there could be a time and a place for a one day class under rare circumstances and only with dedicated and proper mentoring.

However, as it stands currently, one day classes as I have experienced are too prevalent, often abused, and do not start out a new member with the proper tools to improve a candidate as a man. Does that mean we do not get good Masons from a one day class? No, absolutely not. There are hundreds of wonderful Masons who have been products of a one day class. It has been my observation, however, that the men who outshine from a one day class have gone above and beyond to try to earn back what they have missed. I would even argue that these men would have become Masons regardless of the existence of a one day option. Also to be fair, it is worth pointing out that any Mason who was raised in a traditional manner isn't automatically God's gift to Freemasonry simply for showing up for three meetings and repeating an oath.

Earning Freemasonry is something we should all be doing. While one day class members may miss a few symbolic experiences that a traditionally made Mason takes part in, it doesn't change the fact that a new member is a new member is a new member. No man fresh on the sidelines will understand the ins and outs of Freemasonry without proper direction. It is up to you to want to learn it. It is up to you to earn it.

The following pages will hopefully give you an idea of what kind of Mason you are. If you are like me you may even find that you have been MOST of these men at different points in time as you have gone about your way on your Masonic journey. If that is the case you could be well on your way to earning Freemasonry. If not, sit tight and follow me to the end of this book.

Section Two:

Different Freemasons Earning Freemasonry

Section Two:

Different Freemasons Earning Freemasonry

For the New Member

Starting where we all have common ground, you have taken the steps to become a member in good standing. No doubt, you tell yourself shortly after you were raised that you want to learn more. You have just listened to over 10,000 words of dialog and ritual that was interesting, but overwhelming. There is no way you could retain it all, let alone go over in your head what you have just learned.

It is here where you will fall into 1 of 2 categories. Either your Lodge has a really good mentoring program, men to help you out, educational resources, and general Masonic guidance, or another, more common, category of relaxed education, little guidance extended, minimal follow up, and a general lack of caring about the new member once he takes his degree work. If you fall into the latter category it is easy to see why even the most ambitious new Mason can quickly become disheartened and lose interest when he is left to stand alone.

If you have a good mentoring program and helpful leaders, then your battle is half won. You find the resources you need, or at least have enough guidance that you are pointed in the right direction.

If you found that your Lodge has a poor mentoring and follow up program, the rest of this chapter is for you. It is frustrating to find yourself among a bunch of men that seemingly know something you don't about the mysteries of Freemasonry that you have been seeking, but yet you are left with no clue yourself. This is where the first step to earning Freemasonry should be taken. This is where you, as a new member need to take it upon yourself to start asking questions.

One thing that I learned in Freemasonry was that not too many things are going to be handed over to you, and even if they are, you have to want whatever is being given in order for it to work for you. By this, I mean, most Lodge members are not officers and may feel under qualified to give out guidance. Perhaps it is a fear of giving you the wrong answer. Whatever the case, your general attendee may not offer up the support you are looking for unless you ask him a direct question.

I will here remark that if you are a regular attendee who feels unqualified to give guidance, keep reading because there is an entire chapter coming up just for you. Also, by saying that you have to want what is given to you in order for it to work, I mean that it doesn't matter how great the Lodges mentoring program is. You could have the best educators, excellent mentoring, and a list of qualified men 10 pages long and the sad fact remains, sometimes new members are just seeking the card for their wallet. If you are one of these qualified men who have tried in vain to spread the light of Freemasonry but seem to be met with blank faces, I also have a chapter for you, so keep reading.

For the new member, the key is asking questions. Ask any and every question you can about anything you do not understand. Not only will this put you on a path to learning more about the Craft, it can also have the effect of sparking a fire in the existing Lodge members who may not know the answers. We have all sat in a room with a question and NOT asked it because we have been afraid our question was too simple or we would look bad for not knowing it already. The Lodge is no different, we are all human, and sometimes I am relieved when a new member asks a question that I don't know the answer too. That is, as long as he isn't asking ME that question. Even so, what the new member has done in this situation is spread the light of Freemasonry without even knowing it because now two members will learn something new.

It is all about asking questions. Even in the most relaxed Lodges there will be one or two members that know a thing or two about Freemasonry. When you are ready to ask and learn, there WILL be someone there to help you.

Another reality of the new member in today's Freemasonry is the constant and unending stream of digital information right at our fingertips. This is where it is strongly urged to explore, but do so with caution.

The internet is a blessing and a curse of epic proportions when it comes to Freemasonry. Without feeling stupid for asking questions, the new member can turn to the internet to ask any question and explore any part of Freemasonry they wish. Where this fails is when the new member stumbles across the inevitable pit fall of misinformation.

As stated above, any person on this earth can create a blog, social network, website, or other forum to speak freely on any topic they want. These sites may be loaded with information, but too often lack sources and citations. You should never take information as fact, especially when dealing with cross Jurisdiction, unless it is properly sited. A good practice is to trust but verify.

This is especially true when preparing Lodge presentations and speaking engagements. To offer up a simple example of ramped and repeated misinformation, a quick search result on "Famous Freemasons" will produce endless lists of famous American and world figures. Looking at these random unsourced lists I have seen names from Neil Armstrong to Martin Luther King Jr., to Barack Obama. Sometimes these names appear on local and regular Masonic Lodge sites with the best intentions. However, using uncited misinformation like this in a presentation can spread like wildfire around the fraternity.

Keep in mind; this is only one example dealing with a very specific topic. The fraternity isn't going to fall apart if half the members think the first man to walk on the moon was a Freemason. This could, however, impact the fraternity when researching tools of Masonic education such as the working tools.

When it comes to such symbolic items of Masonry, there are few things more important than the working tools of Freemasonry. These simple tools are what make you a Freemason. It is strongly urged that you learn what these tools are and try to use them every single day of your life. While you may find endless information online about the working tools, your number one resource should be no other than the Grand Lodge of your Jurisdiction. The three degrees of Freemasonry teach these to you, but only briefly, and only once. Unless you return to watch or help with degree work or take it upon yourself to dig deeper into the tools, there is no guarantee that they will ever be told to you again. In a perfect world, each Lodge meeting would go over something about these things, but again, our world isn't perfect.

For the new member, one of the first steps you can take to earn Freemasonry is to learn about the working tools. Sometimes, reading about them simply is not enough. Take a few minutes

and look at all of the officers jewels. Come back to Lodge and observe as many degrees as you can. While simply watching them for entertainment CAN become monotonous, keep in mind the degree itself is a learning tool.

Everything done in Freemasonry has a symbolic purpose. From the way we throw our signs, to the way we address each other, and even the way we move about the floor during the degree work is symbolic, and – when appropriately done – builds on the degree work and experience the new brothers are going through.

It's worth pointing out here that just because the Worshipful Master is generally the one doing most of the talking during a degree, that doesn't necessarily make him the ONLY important figure. Observe everyone. Watch the guide closely. Listen to the dialog. Think of questions to ask. If it is in our ritual, it isn't in there by accident. If something doesn't make sense, ask about it.

Searching online is great, but boots on the ground and firsthand experience can be by far a better jump start to Masonic education.

For the Card Carrier

While searching for Masonic information one most likely comes across the phrase, "Freemasonry is the world's oldest and largest fraternity." While this is technically true, what that phrase lets out is the addition of the words "Many of whom never attend a meeting, and cannot tell you very much about the large organization they are a part of." That may sound negative, but the reality is most Freemasons do not attend Lodge meetings. Don't believe me? Find out how many men are officially on your books and then count the attendance at the next meeting. While I am sure there are some very well run observant Lodges that are the exception to the rule, most Lodges are lucky if they see a fraction of their active roles each month.

We need to accept the fact that the card carrier is arguably the most numerous character in our worldwide group. When a Freemason sits in Lodge (assuming he has ever sat in Lodge) we are told in the opening charge of each meeting that we are to remind our brethren of their failings and aid in their reformation. This, my brothers, is my attempt at doing this.

Our membership rolls are stacked to the rafters with men who haven't thought about Freemasonry in years other than paying their dues once a year. Many times these same men are the guys who are getting the final notices and phone calls in April when the dues were due in December. If this is you, LISTEN UP!

While my hope is that a large audience of this book will be the card carriers and ring flashers, in reality, it is not going to be so. It's been my observation that men who have become Masons but haven't taken the time to learn the basics most likely are not going to be picking up an extracurricular book.

However, you are reading this now, that means you at least have some desire to break the mold of your card carrying habits and begin to earn Freemasonry.

The card carriers can have a few different faces. One of these faces affects the fraternity very little. By this, I mean, they do so little with the fraternity that hardly anyone knows they are a member, even the other members. They don't have much to say about it, and generally go about their business just paying their dues and living a Masonically quiet life. These men do not add very much to the Craft, but the important thing here is that they don't take much away from the Craft either.

There is another card carrier that is far more hurtful to the fraternity than the former. This is the glory hound Mason. Most people see this guy a lot. To paint a picture, this is typically the guy who is very open about his Masonic association. Prominently displays the square and compass on his car, ring finger, hat, flag pole, and anywhere else it will fit.

One can usually find this guy talking to non-masons all the time about Freemasonry with stories of George Washington, Ben Franklin, and even the dollar bill. Up until that last part, this guy seemed like no other than just a proud member spreading the joys of the Craft. The last part, however, is where the red flags start to be thrown.

This is the sort of guy who knows so little about the fraternity other than whatever garbage is being spewed on cable TV or some of the aforementioned unsourced websites that when he speaks it actually does nothing but perpetuates the non-truths and misinformation in the fraternity. No doubt this guy sounds like the most educated and dedicated super Mason to all non-Mason he has ever talked to. When this guy is going on and on in a bar or social gathering with his work buddies he really seems to have all the secrets of Freemasonry ready to hand out to anyone who wants to join. What this man doesn't have, however, is the slightest clue what the plumb, level, or square represent. He's most likely never understood the meaning of the working tools; let alone how to apply them to his everyday life.

This same man is the guy who petitions 5 other concordant and appendant bodies of Freemasonry gaining title after title all the while racking up more and more dues payments along the way for meetings he'll never attend, but yet forgets or perhaps doesn't even know the identifying number designation of his own Lodge or chapter.

He is proud to boast about being a 32nd degree Scottish Rite Mason, but other than the one day he showed up to become a Scottish Rite Mason has very little knowledge of what degrees 4-32 actually talk about.

You may ask yourself why I felt the need to paint a picture of the guy we all know exists. To this, I refer back to the main point of this book. If you are this guy, you need to recognize who you are, and then you need to put up, or shut up.

I don't mean, stop being a proud Mason. I mean, unless you have read a book, or sat in Lodge and listened to a program, the odds are, you don't have a clue what you are talking about. For example, any fool with a TV and a computer can tell you George Washington and Ben Franklin were Freemasons, but unless you can take it a step further and add anything more, perhaps keeping your trap shut would be more helpful for the Craft.

The above is not to be assumed that all dedicated Masons know anything at all about George Washington or Ben Franklin as I have put forth. It is to reinforce that paying dues does not make you a Mason, and hardly gives you the right to speak for the fraternity, let alone represent yourself as an authority on any Masonic matter.

Time and time again the attraction of "higher degrees" and different titles is enough to keep dues income steady, but what are you really getting from it?

The true purpose of Freemasonry is self-betterment, not self-absorption. No one ever suggests you should be a quiet Freemason and never talk to your friends about it, but just as in life, if you don't know what you are talking about you probably shouldn't be passing yourself off as an authority.

So, how can this guy earn Freemasonry? Is it too late for this him? As mentioned earlier, if you are reading this it is because you want to earn Freemasonry. At this point if you are one finding yourself flashing your square and compass ring, but you cannot explain what the square and compass symbols represent, then you should probably go back to "For the New Member" and start there. You are essentially a new Mason. You mean well, you are proud, and you want people to know you are a Mason, but you are going about it in all the wrong ways.

Useful knowledge is the great object of our desire. If you do not desire useful knowledge or have not made a single attempt at learning the working tools, how do you expect to live by Freemasonry? Before you can earn Freemasonry you have to accept the fact that Freemasonry is not a civic or social organization.

This society does not exist to serve the community. Believe it or not, we are not supposed to be a group of patriotic men waving flags for the sake of promoting national pride. These things are all side effects that happen because of the lifestyles taught and promoted through Freemasonry.

It is very easy for an uninformed Mason to think that his Lodge should be out there buying groceries for less fortunate, paying heat bills, and donating to charities at every meeting. Yes, these are the stand out actions that we have all witnessed Masons do, but it is hardly what we were required to do. Society is moved by men who give without want, and take less than they are offered. It is actions like this that appear as the public face of Freemasonry. What man wouldn't want to be a part of that?

What is important to understand, however, is that all of this civic action, all of the charity, all of the giving and helping and donating is not done because we are a society expected to do such things. It is done because men who have earned the working tools find themselves automatically doing things like this simply because they are fulfilling their daily obligations as a Freemason.

This notion can create confusion to the uninformed. That brings us to the next card carrier that can be both the silent non-contributor and the glory hound alike. When asked why these men do not attend meetings, they may typically say something along the lines of: "We never do anything." or "I thought we would be helping the elderly and volunteering someplace." So much thought is put into what your Lodge of "the Masons" should be doing that they never realize that "the Mason" can and should be doing all of this stuff on his own.

One does not need to arrive in a van full of Masons at a soup kitchen to volunteer. A Mason should just be doing this sort of thing on his own as his schedule and ability allows. That is, unless you are just in it for the recognition and photo in the "club news" section of the local paper. If this is you, then the Masons are not really who you think they are. Yes, they do volunteer, contribute, donate, and help on occasion, and yes, these photos do end up in the local paper from time to time, but that isn't the overall mission of Freemasonry.

A card carrier can earn Freemasonry in many ways without stepping foot in a Lodge. Becoming informed, and squaring your actions can be the first steps towards self-betterment. If you truly want to be a better Mason the world is full of opportunities to start putting yourself to work. The smallest things like holding a door and saying please and thank you can go a long way to make the world a better place, but it can also start you on a path to self-betterment. To put this into terms of the working tools, use your gavel to start chipping away to your rough edges.

For the Regular Attendee

For some, the obligation to attend meetings every month is something they may take very seriously. For others, there is just a simple joy in going to Lodge every thirty days. Perhaps others just need a few hours away from the house. Month after month they are on time, happy to be there, and also proud to call themselves a Freemason. While not necessarily officers, these men know a few things about what is going on such as what the process is for opening and closing, knowing to say things like "so mote it be" after the prayer and also how to appropriately address the Worshipful Master. They may sign a few petitions and bring a new guy or two in every once in a while. Overall, they are just decent Masons who enjoy coming to Lodge, but don't necessarily want to become involved in the chairs.

These guys sit happy on the sidelines and content with what happens in the meeting. They complain little about how things are run, and some may even fill in a chair when needed. What is it about these guys, then, is there to be improved on? After all, not everyone wants to be an officer.

The desire to come to Lodge is one thing, but many men simply do not have the time commitment to do a stated meeting, plus rehearsals, extra meetings, special communications, school of instruction, or other Masonic things that may pop up. That doesn't make them against learning; it just makes them the average Lodge goer who doesn't want to go any further. It is important to point out here to the rest of us that there should never be an instance where a man is pushed into being an officer or made to feel different for just wanting to sit on the sidelines.

While these men may have already be on the path to earning Freemasonry, that doesn't mean their job is done. It is largely men like this that hold the key to member retention and the feeling of brotherhood. One needs not be Worshipful Master, or any officer for that matter to make a new member feel welcomed. As a matter of fact, it should not be assumed that the officers are the ones solely responsible for growing the Lodge and creating interest for the new members. While it is their duty to lead the Lodge and make sure things are run effectively and on time, it is the entire Lodge body that is responsible to creating the peace and harmony found within its walls. Also, keep in mind, officers are temporary, Lodge members are permanent. Remember, you are the Lodge, without you it doesn't exist. Would you want to come to Lodge if you didn't know anyone, no one sat beside you, or hardly anyone made an effort to talk to you? It's my opinion that no member, new or old, should ever be sitting by himself.

There are plenty of other ways the regular attendee can share the light of Freemasonry. While many things are taught in rehearsal and school of instruction, too often small details such as the correct way to place your hand over your heart during the Pledge of Allegiance (The Sign of Fidelity) or the correct placement of apron strings are the minor details that go undiscussed for years. Many longtime members do not know some of the most basic Masonic courtesies and gestures because they have never been taught. Remember, if you observe anything out of place it is your obligation to aid in correcting it. Simple things like showing others ANYTHING you know is not rude or inappropriate. You don't have to be an officer or even a 24/7 Mason to pass on simple knowledge like this.

Also, much like the card carrier, you must keep in mind that you are not just a Mason while sitting in a Lodge. You are a Mason everywhere you go. One should not just turn off his Masonic practice once he leaves the Lodge. This is where the regular attendee can go the extra mile to earn a little bit more Freemasonry.

If you find yourself already coming to Lodge, why not start taking Lodge with you? Constant refining and self-development is one of the things we should all be doing in Freemasonry while utilizing the working tools. This doesn't mean you have to start volunteering for extra meetings and going to numerous other events. It does mean you are poised to take Freemasonry to the next level by doing just what our closing charge tells you to do; forget not the duties you hear in the Lodge. Be diligent, prudent, temperate, and discreet.

It is here where I want to touch on another type of regular attendee. Much like the former, this man comes to every Lodge meeting and never causes too much of a fuss. What separates this regular attendee from the former is that this man comes seeking light, but may end up finding nothing but shadows.

By this, I mean it is not uncommon for less than entertaining programs, long running minutes, and general disappointment in the way things are being run. While this is an issue that will be covered later in this book, it's important for the regular attendee to not lose heart over this. Easier said than done, right?

While I can sympathize more than anyone on this earth about the frustrations I have driving to Lodge simply to be met with a program that has nothing to do with Freemasonry, or no program at all, there are ways to turn your meeting into an educational experience. This is done through observation and listening.

At the beginning and ending of every single Lodge meeting are the opening and closing charges. These are set in stone and are said every single month. Likewise, our prayers, and dialog are also unchanged. These few things that seem like they are a general waste of time to many are absolutely packed full of Masonic wisdom.

By carefully listening to the dialog of the charges a Mason can create a program for himself simply by trying to take it all in. All members should be doing this, but I'd argue that few actually listen verbatim to the words being said.

This condensed ritual of instruction contains lessons that lay out the purpose of Freemasonry as well as tell you how you are supposed to be living. Even the total lack of a program or a less than perfect display of floor work does not make a wasted meeting. The disgruntled Freemason needs to look at other aspects of the Lodge meeting to appreciate the things that are there, rather than focus on what is missing.

Is this perfect? No. It is not perfect by any stretch of the meaning of the word, but it is helpful, and if you find yourself attending meeting after meeting and not gaining anything, then the best thing for you may be to focus on the items that are being offered freely each month.

For the Officers

There are a million resources that tell you that being officers of the Lodge is a responsibility that should not be taken lightly. While it's worth mentioning here for good measure, the fact remains, thousands of men get pushed into the line, jump into the line, or somehow just end up in the line without giving it much thought about what exactly being an officer should entail.

Once upon a time in Freemasonry the "line" in many Lodges was stocked so well with men wanting the job that typically the Worshipful Master did not have a problem appointing the most qualified men to start in the minor chairs. At the same time, in many of these Lodges, there could exist more than one qualified man campaigning for Worshipful Master. While we still have elections today, the reality is the chair progression pretty much speaks for itself. Most men today can look at their line four years out and be pretty sure who will be Master and when.

Add to this, many Lodges that lack the ambition and commitment of yesterday find themselves simply placing any man who expresses the slightest amount in interest in the minor chairs. This is not always a failure, but it does perpetuate the plague of unqualified men climbing to the top of the ladder before they even know what the ladder is there for, and what you are supposed to do once you get to the top.

Memorizing what you are supposed to say, learning how you are supposed to open the Bible, and figuring out which way to turn when leaving to tile the Lodge can all be learned very easily. Reasons WHY we do these actions the way we do them are often not talked about, and so, not many people in the Lodge really understand the reason behind much of our floor work. It can be frustrating and sometimes comical at the same time if you are the new brother asking, "Why did he do it that way?" and the only answer the seasoned brother has is a shoulder shrug and the reply, "I don't know, it's just the way we have always done it," as the answer. Still, these things are prevalent in the modern Masonic Lodge.

What is important for the officers to understand is that we never do something just because that is the way we have always done it. Almost every single action, step, and sign in our Lodge has a very specific reasoning behind it. If you find that you are one of the men who answers with a shoulder shrug, then you, my brother, are missing out on much of what our meeting should be offering you. Just like in life, if you are doing anything but have no idea why you are doing it, you probably aren't gaining much of anything from it. If you get nothing out of being an officer, odds are, you won't be able to give much in return.

Take being an officer serious. There are many guys who rely on you, even in the minor chairs. The Worshipful Master, Senior and Junior Wardens all have a job to do, but that job is not to do everyone's job. It can be seen often in Lodges where the minor officers are relaxed about the position they are appointed to, and as a result, may not show up for degree conferrals, or may not take time to learn the appropriate steps and ways to conduct themselves at their station in the Lodge. At the same time, the main officers appoint men without giving it too much thought, and as a result, find they are light on officers on meeting night.

New officers should be treated much like new members. They have no idea what they are doing many times. It takes guidance, direction, and mentoring. If you, as Master, are only wrapped up in going over your degree work on rehearsal night, then the minor officers will quickly lose interest. Every rehearsal meeting should include at least something for everyone. While many times there is someone going over his degree, in the grand scheme of things, this may not be the MOST appropriate place to hold 8 other men hostage with nothing to do but listen.

On the other hand, if you are one of these minor officers going to rehearsal and not being utilized, then it is your job to make the most of it, much like the regular attendee at a meeting, the things that are being spoken and rehearsed, even if they aren't your part or dialog, are extremely important for you to understand as early as you can, especially if you are going to be advancing in the line.

Earning Freemasonry for the officers is a bit different than earning Freemasonry for the general membership. Unlike the general membership, you've accepted a role that requires you to be involved. Of course this starts with asking questions, but it also requires you to do a little bit outside of Lodge.

As mentioned above, sometimes men find themselves railroaded into officer positions. If this is the case with you, you may not even want to take steps to earn Freemasonry. However, if you took the position knowingly and wanting to be an officer, then you at least have some desire to improve. The goal for you should be to take this initial desire and build on it.

If you find yourself being underutilized or at least not getting what you desire out of it, then you need to speak up. Like every level, if you want to know something, ask. If you don't understand something, ask. If you are curious about something, speak up and let your voice be heard. Remember, you are an officer, people will look to you for answers. If all your answers are shoulder shrugs it probably won't do much to spread the light of Freemasonry to other up and comers.

All Grand Lodges have resources available. It's also been my experience that most Lodges have little clue of these resources outside of the secretary or Worshipful Master. Secretaries hold the key to many resources and Grand Lodge communications.

They are also in the same position for years on end while the Worshipful Master is only a temporary fixture in the east.

Year after year, the secretaries can become self-involved autocracies in many aspects. It is a thankless job that many men do not realize takes a significant amount of out-of-the-Lodge personal time. It's no wonder that after planning, recording, minute taking, dues paying, book keeping, organizing, and everything else that is involved in the role of secretary that he isn't also holding the hand of the membership to lead them to the resources passed to him by Grand Lodge.

Secretaries receive many things from their Grand Lodge. Some of these things are minor and some are major. The secretary on occasion has to take liberties or paraphrase correspondence instead of reading verbatim what is to be passed to the brethren. The autocracy comes in when important things are left out, or are paraphrased down to "…if you want more information, it's on my desk." This is hardly done for spite or malice, but the fact is, sometimes much of the correspondence can be monotonous and time wasting. By stating that resources are "on my desk" it covers the necessary topics, while putting the ball in the member's court. If the brethren want more info, the brethren may come get it.

While this is technically the case, in reality what happens is that it is often forgotten about by the end of the meeting. Even if it is not, there always seems to be a flood of folks around the secretary after the meeting with far more pressing issues than you wanting to know where to find the verbatim correspondence of the last meeting of Academy of Masonic Knowledge. It can be intimidating. Because of this intimidation, useful information falls into the bottomless pit that is the secretary's records.

Still, you as an officer need to listen to the minutes. See what they have to say, as boring as it may be. As a suggestion, one of the most useful tools that I ever started using in Lodge is a pen and small pad in my front pocket. It is good practice to help keep tabs on specific dates and times that the secretary speaks about during the meeting. It can also be helpful in numerous other ways that can make you as a member stand out.

For example, when I sat in any chair as an officer, or even on the sidelines as a general attendee, each month someone is recognized about something. Maybe there is a birthday. Maybe there are a few visitors. Maybe there is a very good speaker. Often times when these men are recognized, they stand, speak their piece, thank the Worshipful Master for the recognition, and sit back down. This is typically the end of the story. However, knowing the names of these men at the end of the meeting can be a simple gesture that goes a long way to the men who were recognized. When, or if in some cases, the Worshipful Master asks if any of the brethren have anything additional to offer, knowing those names can make these visitors and presenters feel appreciated yet again.

A simple, "I want to say it is nice to have brothers Tom, Fred, and Bill here tonight. It's always nice meeting new faces," or "Brother Frank, that was an excellent presentation," can go a long way.

Go up to anyone you just learned the name of after a meeting and shake their hand with a real general appreciation. This is the unwritten part of being an officer. You may not have much to do or much responsibility as some of the other officers, but you are still representing the men who run the Lodge.

For the Past Masters

As you move along your Masonic path you will find that there is no clear end point to the Craft. This is a lifelong commitment that you will work at no matter how far you have gone in Freemasonry. Moving through your year in the east can be an overwhelming time. You aren't necessarily expected to have all the answers, but it is your behind on the line when things fall apart.

Like the other officers, the rule of Worshipful Master is one not to be taken lightly. You need to put more than 100% effort into it. You need to give until you cannot give any more to do it correctly and successfully. At the end of the year, if you are in a Lodge like most, you get a nice shiny jewel for a job well done.

To find out what kind of Master you are, or have been, ask yourself one question: Did you serve to earn a jewel, or did you serve to earn Freemasonry? Too often we see today a halfhearted attempt at serving as Master. There are a few things to think about during your year. Did you over rely on your minor officers? Did you miss meetings without notice? Did you make any attempt to reach out to the brethren other than the monthly notice that the secretary most likely prepared? How were your programs? When you left Lodge did you do anything at all Masonic until the next meeting?

Maybe you did everything above with pride and dedication to the fullest, maybe you did not. The fraternity is full of wonderful Worshipful Masters, but there is also no shortage of bad Masters either. In the end, though, you will be a Past Master whether you deserve it or not. Congratulations, here is your jewel. You can hang it from your breast. What happens then?

Growing as a man and Freemason doesn't end when you get done with your year in the East. In many ways, it is only the beginning. As exclusive of a club as the Masons are supposed to be, the Past Masters club is even a bit more exclusive. You are not just a member; you are not even an officer. You are now part of the local Lodge's elite. Once a year for the rest of your life your lapel pin collection grows by one and there is a dinner in your honor. It is up to you earn this status by maintaining your connection to the Lodge.

Many Masters feel like they have been there and done that. It's now time to take a break and sit back. With fewer meetings and almost no responsibility anymore you think you can have some time to just enjoy the show.

Do the Lodge a favor and smack that nonsense out of your head right now. You can relax, but don't retire. I find effective Past Masters, and ones that are generally respected more are ones that touch base with the Master and officers outside of the Lodge. As a Past Master you want to care about how your former Lodge is run, but at the same time you cannot step on the new Masters toes. It is his will and pleasure how things are run, so on meeting night, just sit tight. Let the Lodge do its thing. Of course there will be things you would not do, but that doesn't make them incorrect.

The key to being a successful Past Master in my opinion is being accessible to the brethren. Advertise your willingness to help out. At the same time don't steal any of the officer's thunder. Maybe this new group doesn't want your help. That is ok too. It's not your Lodge anymore.

Given your exclusive status as a Past Master you must also remain as grounded as you can. While you did do something wonderful, remember, you are still just a member. Be sure to sit among the brethren. While not the case everywhere, in some Lodges it has become practice that Past Master have an unofficial Past Master's section or at least a general gravitation for such men to sit in the same general area. This can be standoffish to some of the brethren. A feeling of, "Well, I guess I can't sit there, they are exclusive," can result from this.

Sitting among the brethren reassures the Lodge members that you see yourself as just one of them. This concept of being on the level is one of the basic tenets of Freemasonry. It provides the membership easy access to the guys who may have more answers, and it removes the intimidation of barrier and approach.

When you seek the office of Worshipful Master, you aren't just serving a year. You are taking a commitment of leadership for the rest of your life. The brethren did not have to vote for you, but they did, so earn it.

Past Masters are also the men who are expected to know everything. I will be the first to admit, I do not know everything. This is one of the main reasons to continue to not only come to meetings as often as possible, but to also continue my Masonic education.

The resources, books, bylaws, constitutions, and other Grand Lodge resources that are available to all members should be a familiar site to you. Sure, as you get further away from your time in the East you will forget some, but you cannot completely let go of everything you have ever learned.

Here is where you almost have the opportunity to pick your favorite aspect of Freemasonry and throw yourself into it. In my Lodge, and I am sure many other Lodges, we have a few older Past Masters who have not conferred a degree in twenty years, but when asked could perform a near flawless degree on the spot. There are other Past Masters who may not be so sharp on the degree work, but who have a very good knowledge of the working tools and how they are to be used. Likewise, there are also men who go on to help with hall associations and secretary type duties. As an individual you can't be expected to know and do all of this, but as a whole, your group of Past Masters, it is your job to show off your strengths to the brethren. Set an example. Guide in the right direction. Share your experiences and remind the brethren of what you can do from time to time.

For the Committed

So far I have laid out how I view the Craft through various types of members. Up to this point I have done this all through my personal experience. You, like me, may have found yourself in many of these same positions during your Masonic career. If you have gone from stage to stage and find yourself a washed up old has-been Past Master, you may be wondering what else you can do. Perhaps you are not a Past Master, and have no desire to be one. There are still many ways you can become the stand out Mason that people turn to for questions.

If you are committed to Freemasonry, being a Past Master is only a minor step in your Masonic Career. Sure it gives you a little bit of clout, but there is much more you can do if you want to continue to improve.

While this book is not about learning Freemasonry, that doesn't take away the fact that you do need to learn it in order to earn it. While not all people who learn Freemasonry earn it, it is impossible to earn it without learning it.

Learn every possible thing you can about the Craft. There is no one path to take. Some men learn history. Some men learn philosophy. Some men learn the ritual. The resources available on most Grand Lodge websites, or at your Grand Lodge itself, are endless. Reprints of many Grand Lodge minutes can be found online too.

Read. Read everything you can get your hands on. This means general things like the notices, Grand Lodge publications and correspondence. Read them cover to cover. There are many real gems hidden right in the open.

While you are reading, why not start writing. One way to give back to the fraternity is to be a resource that shares experiences when asked. Wouldn't it make sense then to share your opinions and knowledge by writing them down for all to read, retain, reference, study, and contemplate?

Most Grand Lodges have a magazine or publication. These are excellent resources to start submitting your work to. Contact the editors. Pass a few pieces to your District Deputy. Offer up a program for your Lodge. Do you know how many Lodges are dying for a great presenter or program?

If you feel your Lodge is boring, don't just sit there and wait for it to not be. Get to work creating a program. It's almost guaranteed in most Lodges that if you approach the Worshipful Master with a program he will allow you to do it at some point.

Along the lines of researching what your Grand Lodge offers, be sure to look into Lodges of Research and Masonic Academies. Most Jurisdictions have some sort of educational body that will meet annually or biannually. These meetings can be an excellent place to broaden your Masonic horizons. It is one thing to read a Masonic book. It is another thing to actually meet Masonic authors and scholars.

In the Jurisdiction of Pennsylvania, for example, there exists both a Lodge of Research and a Masonic Academy. These bodies meet bi-annually and typically have men from all around the state in attendance. They are bodies that value the ancient landmarks of the fraternity and send members on the correct path in Freemasonry.

While dues can be an issue, some of these bodies, like the Pennsylvania Academy of Masonic Knowledge, are simply institutes with personal achievement and Masonic education programs free of charge. Adding to this, the requirements for advancement are largely based on reading and evaluating books that are freely available from the Grand Lodge library and you have a recipe for unlimited Masonic growth, all at no or very little cost.

Knowing your options and resources can be the difference between stagnant membership with no personal life improvement and the Masonic light switch that suddenly turns on and changes your life forever.

Section Three:

Where are we Headed?

Modern Trends

Another modern way to give back what you have earned is through social media and online Masonic networking. More and more today we are seeing men connecting with each other to share ideas and stories. While there is no lack of garbage out there, you can use many free resources to create your own Masonic world.

Emerging technology and modern resources are making it easier and easier to share and discuss our fraternity with each other.

Our fraternity is full of men from all different walks of life. This is nothing new. However, along with changing demographics come the introduction of modern technology and the emerging "instant gratification" generation taking over.

We have to face facts that the Greatest Generation is disappearing and times just aren't the same any more. Where once in a bygone era a Lodge meeting or degree work was seen as not only educational, but also entertaining, today we are faced with unlimited other forms of entertainment. We simply don't look to fraternal orders for entertainment and self-betterment the same way it was done in the past.

Throughout this book we've also addressed a few of the too often seen problems in modern Freemasonry and how they have changed our order. In an era of the internet, social media, and a generation of men who are all too used to instant gratification, hopefully this book will help you uncover a few things about the Craft that have fallen by the wayside. With any luck, you will discover which kind of Mason you are and start on the path to earning Freemasonry. It is this author's hope that this book will either help you in your Masonic development or aid in your restoration.

While there are literally millions of research options out there, it is important to tread carefully in the mess that can be online. The misinformation out there can swallow up a new Mason or uninitiated petitioner.

The misinformation or skewed information out there can seem like it is far more in your face and accessible than the legitimate information. If you aren't an involved Mason, or are new to masonry, most likely you haven't been heavily exposed to official Masonic resources such as minutes and reprints. This is especially true if you are happy to be a Mason, but don't find yourself inside the walls of the Lodge very often.

Misinformation seems to be produced and promoted by far more vocal groups than many of our own local Lodges. Members turning to the internet to find quick tidbits of information COULD find some real gems. At the same time, it's more likely they will stumble across unsourced, uncited, and downright incorrect information.

Every anti-Mason and conspiracy theorist with a computer can produce thousands of hours of non-truths and downright garbage. Many times these blogs, sites, sermons, and commentary use no original sources or citations, or when they do they grossly distort the facts by cherry picking lines of text out of context. Add to this many clandestine and irregular bodies passing themselves off as legitimate Freemasonry and you find yourself in a web of confusion.

Facebook and social media has given every man with an interest an instant connection with thousands of men of the same interest. Starting a blog to share your Masonic thoughts can gain a following of men that will help your grow your Masonic experiences to epic proportions.

When you share with your Lodge you always run the risk that the guys you are sharing with really don't care about what you are saying. When you have a new "like" on Facebook it is generally because the audience is appreciative of what you have to say.

Connecting with your favorite authors, scholars, and bloggers online can keep you in the loop of all things Masonic over many Jurisdictions. I can personally attest to the benefits of social media because I myself have done this.

Starting with a simple blog and one follower I was able to post a general blog about Freemasonry. I used the same username to create a promotional Facebook page where I can connect with other bloggers who write things I find interesting. Before long I found that not only was there people who genuinely wanted to hear what I had to say, but that were also commenting and creating a dialog of thoughts and ideas that built off what I was posting about.

These men, you will find out, are much like you. They are tech savvy enough to find their way to your blog. These men, if engaged in dialog, can act almost like a substitute for what you are missing in Lodge. As mentioned in the previous pages it can be frustrating when it seems like you are the only one in your Lodge who cares enough about Masonic education to spend time on it. Social media takes this frustration and places you with like-minded men.

Personal blogs about Freemasonry are popping up at a rapid rate. These can be read, reread, and discussed for far longer periods than the hour you spend once a month in Lodge.

While this is in no way a substitution for going to Lodge, it can give you an outlet to find and associate with the men who share your particular interest. Some men love talking about the esoteric side of Masonry. There is a page for that. Some men like talking about Masonic history. There is a page for that.

Some men like talking about charity and social functions. There are pages for that.

While Lodge holds many secrets, much about Freemasonry can be shared with the public. Because of this, as long as you are not speaking ritual or giving away the landmarks, an ambitious writer could find that he is a new resource for non-Masons looking into the Craft.

With all the garbage out there having a legit source of personal experience can benefit both the Craft and the light seeker. If you chose to do this route it is always a good idea to cite, reference, and give credit to any source that you use for information. This is just simple common courtesy.

Using the modern ways to connect and share online can lead you to creative development for Lodge presentations as well. While going online and using social networking is not for everyone, it doesn't change the fact that through one member utilizing it as a source, the online community can affect even the most old school Lodge. Men are bouncing ideas off each other, gathering facts, putting together programs and helping each other share the light across hundreds of miles.

These projects can be taken to local Lodges anywhere in the world to be shared with the brethren.

That's Too Much to Learn!

One of the most common answers a member will give when asked why they don't want to do more is the old response of, "That's too much to learn." This is partially true. Not everyone can memorize the floor work, let alone several thousand lines of flawless ritual. The intimidation of memorizing the ritual can stop a man's desire even before he attempts to learn it.

What is important to understand is that there are only a few men in the Lodge each year that are required to know the ritual. The rest are all supporting roles. You do not have to memorize the ritual right away to understand Freemasonry.

Actually, if you are starting out, memorizing the ritual is the last thing that should be on your mind in my opinion. Gaining an understanding of the working tools and simple things that are readily available from Lodge sources is a great place to start.

Building from there, if one desires, it can be easy to transition to minor roles such as guiding candidates during degree work, prayers, minor chairs, and other less involved, but equally important roles. The simple act of opening the Bible correctly is a huge help and doesn't even require memorized dialog in most Jurisdictions.

The minor roles will help you understand why we do things instead of just doing them because the guys above you told you to. When you skip a few chairs or jump to quickly in line you run the risk of continuing the trend of just getting by.

One thing that I realized when I started learning the degree work for Junior Warden certification is that all of the minor roles that I did prior to that paid off big time. While the degree work was intimidating to look at on the surface, once I got down to it I found that many of those minor roles had repeating portions show up in the Junior Warden dialog.

Of course there is still more to learn, but having three or four lines of text thrown in here and there that you already know from previous jobs helps not only to reduce the dialog you need to memorize, but also works as markers or milestone points when you are reciting in Lodge.

This same concept goes for the Senior Warden and Worshipful Master. Once a man learns a degree, the others generally become a little bit easier to retain while learning. Building upon what you have learned to make a better finished product is what Masonry is all about. Learning things the correct way first goes a long way to earning it in the long run.

In this book we have covered the new members, card carriers, regular attendees, officers, and Past Masters. All of these men have an obligation to learn various aspects of Freemasonry. Each of these men should be learning different aspects with varying degrees of importance. What is amazing about it all is that the further you travel in Freemasonry you will find that it all comes together.

How do I know if I have Earned It?

Throughout this book, in more than one way, I have said that just because you learn it, doesn't mean you have earned it. Freemasonry is full of men who learn steps, signs, rituals, and floor work without ever understanding any of it. Since most Jurisdictions have a requirement to advance or hold a particular office, sometimes these advancements are bastardized by men who rush to memorize everything without truly understanding.

In any Lodge there exist men who can tell you word for word, line for line what the ritual is, but when you ask them to just speak of the story of Hiram Abiff and the Temple they have no clue where to start. Likewise, there are men who don't so much as have a prayer or opening charge memorized but can tell you exactly how Freemasonry affects their daily lives. They understand the working tools and the landmarks and customs of the fraternity.

Even without holding an office or station, these men are the men who are earning Freemasonry. Arguably the men that understand Masonry and use it every day can be more beneficial to the order than even the highest officer if a said officer is just floating through the chairs. While earning Freemasonry doesn't require that you stand out or ever have your name on a plaque in the Lodge, it does require that you aren't just a bystander. In a perfect world there would be no freeloaders or bystanders in Freemasonry.

Staring your Masonic education as a new member and continuing long after you are a Past Master will not just improve you as a Freemason, but will also improve all that is around you.

Our system exists because it works. For hundreds of years there have been millions of members. While the Craft has moved away from its true purpose, the true roots of the organization are still there. It is up to all of us to blow off the dust and start using the tools again.

You will know if you earned Freemasonry when you start seeing the tools work. Finding yourself wanting to give instruction, thinking about ways to improve your life, offering Masonic guidance and finding yourself constantly looking to the working tools to make daily decisions are pretty good indicators that you have successfully earned at least a portion of Freemasonry.

The wonderful thing about the order, in my opinion, is that there is no cap on the personal benefits of the order. If you see an improvement in your life simply because you chose a tool and tried to live by it, then perhaps it is time to pick another tool and start using it.

Using the 24 inch gauge can help you symbolically divide your time between work, family, and rest. It simple, you have to go to work even if you don't want to. While you are there, give 8 good hours to work. You need to have family life and time for your faith and devotion. Give 8 hours to those items. You need to rest. Give 8 hours of rest.

Knowing the lessons of the level can help you become a more rounded person. You can find yourself being open to other thoughts and ideas. You find yourself not intimidated by others who are above you, but focus on the reality that we are all equal and all have the same opportunity to work for what we want.

Some people get a free pass. That's life, forget them! If you want something, go for it. No one but yourself can stop you.

The gavel is another simple and powerful tool that we all need to be using. What are your bad habits? Maybe they don't hurt anyone. So what! Maybe they aren't helping anything either. Do you swear too much? Do you get road rage? Do you drink or smoke too much? The gavel isn't meant to transform you instantly into a perfect person, but with a little chip here and there if will surely help you improve over time.

These are just a few of the examples you can and should be using the many working tools of the Lodge. They aren't just symbols placed there to look pretty. They are tools for our lives. Use them!

Sharing It

The great secrets of Freemasonry are not a handshake and a password. Anyone can find this stuff online. That does not make you a Freemason. A member can witness a degree in Lodge 100 times and still not understand what is happening. This is where perhaps one of the best ways a man can continue to earn Freemasonry is the simple act of sharing it. I don't mean sharing the same things he can find on his own, but sharing his views and opinions and interpretations of it.

The simplest things that you have stored away in your head can change someone's life. As you learn to use Freemasonry in your life, no doubt, it will start to improve. For many, one day it just clicks, and all the time you spent memorizing ritual and learning floor work and hailing signs can become very insignificant. When you discover the true power of Freemasonry you will realize that it has been in front of you the entire time.

Don't keep that to yourself. Sadly, many people never have the "ah ha" moment. Our duties to our brethren are much like the duties to ourselves. We are to help one another and guide each other to better lives and lifestyles. Sharing what you know is just another way of performing your duty as a Freemason.

Of course, sharing the light of Freemasonry is not just limited to your brethren in the Lodge. The entire world today can seem corrupt, scary, unwelcoming, and just plain negative at times. When you couple that with the fact that many people, including our own members, do not understand what Freemasonry is or why we exist in the first place, it becomes clear that we need to work harder at sharing the light to more people than just the members.

While I have mentioned before, it is worth repeating; Freemasonry is about making you a better person. Using the working tools in your daily lives will, by default, help you become a stand out person. While we aren't a society that exists simply to do charity, the fact remains you will be a more charitable person. While we aren't a society that exists to donate and money to relief projects, the fact remains, you will be doing more of this sort of thing by default. There is nothing wrong with crediting the fraternity for your actions if, in fact, the fraternity is the reason you felt moved to do good deeds.

You shouldn't necessarily tell people that you are doing things on behalf of the Freemasons. Instead, you should always feel free to say you do things because you are a Freemason.

The world misunderstands our Fraternity. No one except us can fix that. By exemplifying nothing but the best you can be we can improve the image of Freemasonry worldwide.

On a smaller scale, by exemplifying and sharing nothing but the best you can be we can improve our own local Lodges. It is up to no one but us to start this process in our own lives.

What about a Mason at Sight?

One often misunderstood act in Freemasonry is that of being made a Mason at site. So many in our fraternity misunderstand this topic to such a high degree that it is often difficult for members to find exactly what it means.

While in discussion one day with a few brethren about the effectiveness of one day classes and Masons made at site I realized that this topic was not just misunderstood, but also controversial because of the misunderstanding. As luck would have it I was at that time trying to think of a topic for my final paper for the Pennsylvania Academy of Masonic Knowledge. Because this topic goes hand in hand with the subject matter of this book I have decided to include it here in its entirety with sources. You can also find this and much more on my blog at www.squareofvirtue.wordpress.com.

Hopefully, after reading this, you will understand the origins and regularity of this practice. You should also understand what separates this practice for the one day classes.

A Mason at Sight

The Rare Special Event with Common Misconceptions
Adam T. Osman - Final Research Paper
Pennsylvania Academy of Masonic Knowledge

A phrase that seems to appear from time to time is "Mason at Sight." For many Masons and non-Masons alike this conjures up images of the Grand Master waving his hand like a wizard and saying something along the lines of, "ABRA KA-DABRA...IT IS DONE." The result being an ordinary man is instantly titled Master Mason without any effort or knowledge of the Craft.

There is no shortage of misinformation out there on the process of being made a Mason at sight. The term itself implies that with one pen stroke the Grand Master takes a man and declares him a Freemason. This could not be further from the truth.

In fact, when a Grand Master makes a Mason at sight, it is not too extremely different from our widely accepted one day classes. Of course there are certain differences that exist between Jurisdictions, but for the most part being made a Mason at sight is not as much of a free pass that many people claim.

The actual process of making a Mason at sight is common but rare. As of 2011, in Pennsylvania, this has only happened 91 times since 1842.[1] Often times these special events are very large ceremonies attended by many members to witness the degree work in its entirety as was the case in 1998 when three Pennsylvania State Police officers were raised to the Sublime degree of a Master Mason by the Pennsylvania State Police Masonic Degree Team.[2] *(degree team since dissolved)*

With the Grand Masters approval, a Mason at sight event can be more than just degree work by any ordinary members. Many times special degree teams made up of men from specific lines of work make it not only a special event for the candidates involved, but also displays the various special interest degree teams recognized by the Grand Jurisdiction of Pennsylvania. As mentioned above the Pennsylvania State Police Masonic Degree team was just one of the various degree teams. Pennsylvania also hosts the Pennsylvania Masonic Emergency Services Degree Team which took part in a similar event in 2002 when two men of the emergency services profession were made Masons at sight.

3

In Pennsylvania, the Grand Master has the authority as the chief Masonic official in the Jurisdiction to make a man a Mason without the traditional process of petitioning a Lodge, submitting to an investigation of his background, or awaiting the outcome of a Lodge vote. In addition, the candidate does not have to wait a month in between degrees. [4]

Although it is becoming more common than ever for one day conferrals and mass initiations, especially in Pennsylvania, there are differences between the so called 'One Day Classes" and being made a Mason at sight. During an official one day class, each candidate has gone through the exact preparation as a traditional candidate. He has filed a petition seeking the prayer of his petition to be granted. The petition was signed by two Master Masons as recommenders. The petition is brought before the Lodge for the approval or rejection of the candidate's prayer being granted, and then upon approval, the candidate is interviewed by a committee of three Master Masons. Upon a report to the Lodge on the candidate, the Lodge votes to approve or reject the candidate for membership. If approved, the candidate then moved through three degrees of the symbolic

Lodge either in a traditional format of one degree at a time, or in a one day event receiving all three degrees one after the other.

When a man is made a Mason at sight, he still takes the degree work the same as any candidate would. The differences lie in the fact that the Grand Master can vouch for the character of the man in question, and therefore forgo the petition, ballot, and interview process. The candidate still takes his full degree work, complete with charges and investiture. [5]

Typically a Mason at sight is someone of high regard or otherwise a pillar of society. Just a few noted men who have become Masons at sight in Pennsylvania include Samuel W. Pennypacker (1897), Governor of Pennsylvania; John Wanamaker (1898), Merchant; Andrew and Richard Mellon (1928), Financiers; Milton S. Eisenhower (1951), brother of President Dwight Eisenhower; George M. Leader (1955), Governor of Pennsylvania; Fitz Eugene Dixon, Jr. (1976), Philanthropist; and Col. Paul J. Evanko (1999), Pennsylvania State Police Commissioner.[6]

The record for most Masons made at sight by a Pennsylvania Grand Master is nine. It is held by Grand Master Benjamin Page who was in office from 1932 -1933.He is followed by William A. Carpenter with 7 between 1984 and 1985. Tied for third are Grand Masters William J. Kelley (1897-1898) and J. Wilson Smith (1928-1929) each with 5.[7]

The earliest accounts, according to Mackey's Encyclopedia, include an instance of Lord Lovell making the Duke of Lorraine, who later became Emperor of Germany, a Mason at sight in 1731. Mackey also tells us that the Duke of Gloucester was made a Mason at sight in 1766. The Duke of Cumberland received this honor in 1767. In 1787, in an "occasional Lodge" the Prince of Wales was made a Mason at sight. The term "occasional Lodge" can also be called "emergency Lodge" which Mackey tells us is; "specially convened by him (The Grand Master), and consisting of such Master Masons as he may call together for that purpose only; the Lodge ceasing to exist as soon as the initiation, passing, or raising has been accomplished, and the Brethren have been dismissed by the Grand Master."[8]

Although the practice of making Masons at sight had been recorded in some form or another as early as 1731, it did not become officially authorized in Pennsylvania until 1825. In this year an addition of the "Ahiman Rezon" was printed that listed one of the Grand Masters powers; *"To cause Masons to be made in his presence, at any time; and at any place, a Lodge being opened by him for that purpose."*[9]

As of 1995, the authority was expanded to read as; *"To cause Masons to be made in his presence, at any time and at any place, a Lodge being opened by him for that purpose; To grant, and authorize to be granted, Dispensations for making Masons, for constituting Lodges, for laying Cornerstones, for forming Masonic processions, and for the burial of unaffiliated Master Masons; Adopted December 6, 1995*[10]*"*

It is also worth noting that a man made a Mason at sight still has to petition an individual Lodge for acceptance. So while a few steps in the process have been relaxed with the approval, supervision, and direction of the Grand Master, these men still need to ballot a Lodge for membership. Unlike the one day classes when a man is made a member of a Lodge while typically sitting beside many men who are becoming members of different Lodges, Masons at sight, many times, are just made Masons of that particular Jurisdiction. A Lodge still has to accept his prayer of his petition for membership. This is similar to a membership transfer.

As stated in the current Ahiman Rezon; 19.04. *"Brethren made at sight or by Dispensation do not thereby become members of the Lodge in which they are made. To become members they must apply by petition, and be duly elected, as hereinafter provided."*[11]

The idea that making a Mason at sight is somehow bad or negative to Freemasonry is nothing new. Many authors have touched on this topic for years. While it is worth noting this practice has been around for many years, some Jurisdictions have claimed they forbid it, but at the same time actually performing it in practice. One noted Masonic author, Albert G. Mackey, touched on this topic in 1874;

The prerogative of the Grand Master to make masons masons at sight, is a Landmark which is closely connected with the preceding one. There has been much misapprehension in relation to this Landmark, which misapprehension has sometimes led to a denial of its existence in Jurisdictions where the Grand Master was perhaps at the very time substantially exercising the prerogative, without the slightest remark or opposition...[12]

The misleading title of "Mason at sight" has caused many uneducated members to hold animosity towards such an action. While it only takes a few minutes of searching online or browsing Grand Lodge records to prove otherwise, there still exist the thought that a member is somehow less a member because he was made a Mason at sight. Indeed, there is typically discussion among brethren when referring to our Masonic presidents that often times leads to at least one person pointing out that President Taft was made a Mason at sight, and for that reason was less a real Mason and more of an honorary Mason.

In reality, not only did Taft receive the entire three degree ritual in person, but also went on to witness other men complete their

Masonic journey in the Master Mason degree. When Taft received his degrees at the Scottish Rite Cathedral in Ohio in 1909, the Grand Lodge of Ohio had already been performing the Mason at Sight ritual for some time. [13]

So often was the notion of "Mason at Sight" misunderstood with a negative connotation that from time to time some Grand Masters would issue statements on such proceedings. As we can read from Maryland Grand Master Thomas J. Shryock in 1897:

By virtue of the authority in me vested as your Grand Master, I convened an Emergency Lodge, and made, "at sight," His Excellency, Lloyd Lowdes, Governor of Maryland, a Mason. An erroneous idea has arisen in the minds of many of the fraternity as to the ceremony if making a Mason 'at sight,' and to erase this wrong, and perhaps damaging impression, I deem it but proper to sat that, in the making of a mason 'at sight,' by the Grand Master, the candidate is required to pass through all the forms and ceremonies incident to the conferring of the Three Degrees, in the same manner that an applicant does in applying to a subordinate Lodge. The impression of some that the Grand

Master, by virtue of his authority, touches a man on the shoulder and creates him a mason is entirely erroneous and I know that this impression does exist to a certain extent. I think it proper to here state, so the Craft may understand it throughout our Jurisdiction, that such is not the case. The making of a Mason 'at sight,' is one of the landmarks of the Fraternity, the prerogative of the Grand Master, and I have on two occasions exersized that prerogative, as much for the purpose of not allowing it to become dormant as for any other reason."[14]

One thing to take from the above clarification made by Grand Master Shryock is that it would seem a defense added to the use of such a ceremony would be the claim that it must be used in order for it to continuously be understood. While to some that may seem like a fancy way of politicking the situation, it is very true. As we see too often in Lodges as men move though the chairs, become Master, and move on to bigger and better things, many times the members holding the reins are only educated in what they have personally seen or took part in. Any ritual, extra floor work, or otherwise seldom used ceremony that is not constantly utilized it often lost to the next generation of men.

For proof of this, I can attest with my own personal knowledge that when Grand Lodge officially allowed stated meetings to be opened and closed in the short way; [15] what at first seemed like a harmless shortcut became a matter of many new members not seeing the long form traditional opening or closing for up to 2 years. These same men who had never seen the work performed were clueless when asked to do it in ritual. As easy as it is for some to say, "Attend school of instruction." The reality is, if you don't use it, you lose it.

What is also important to remember is that each Jurisdiction is subject to no one except the Grand Master of their own Jurisdiction. While this practice has been seen as controversial, it is also widely practiced across the world each year. In fact, our own "One Day Class" events that are held by dispensation of the Grand Lodge of Pennsylvania in which large numbers of men are made Masons in a one day auditorium type event are very similar in practice.

It is worth noting that those who decry the practice of making Masons at sight, but seem to acknowledge the practice of one day classes are obviously blindly ignorant to what exactly this practice is. In fact, the one day class ritual could be seen as more detrimental to the Craft, as each candidate is not led individually through the degree, but rather sits among many other men viewing it from a chair.

The growing popularity of one day Masonic classes is not in itself met without controversy. One does not have to ask around for very long before they realize that there stands a silent but constant negative aura of feelings between some members of the fraternity. While there is never an official designation of who is or is not a traditional candidate, one day Masons do face scrutiny from time to time.

The rising popularity of one day events has paved the way for a more general acceptance of this practice, although it is up for debate as to its effectiveness on productive membership. There are arguments to be made on both sides of the aisle.

What is clear however is that there is no shortage of highly dedicated men claiming the ranks of Past Master or other officers of the Lodge who are products of the one day classes. It would seem that no matter how a man is made a Mason, if he, individually, chooses to pursue the path to Masonic enlightenment he will achieve his goals, even with negative and unnecessary hurdles in his way.

Another hurdle that appears from time to time is cross Jurisdiction recognition. As is the case in any Grand Jurisdiction, each Grand Master technically answers to no person outside his Jurisdiction. While many states vary slightly in certain aspects of ritual, practice, or work, for the most part they all maintain the same landmarks and mutual respect. This allows each Grand Master to govern his Jurisdiction accordingly while maintaining harmony and recognition of other Jurisdictions. On occasion, a Grand Master may perform a dispensation that goes contrary to what most other Grand Masters would feel is acceptable.

There is a long-standing legend among many Prince Hall Masons that Dr. Martin Luther King Jr. was made a Mason at sight posthumously in 1999 in Georgia. As is typical online, once this is posted, or reposted, emotions run wild with men from both sides both in support and adamantly against this notion. As it turns out, this legend is false. Dr. King was never made a Mason in life, nor posthumously. Not to mention the shear notion of this action would go contrary to the landmarks of the fraternity.

Although this notion may seem far fetch and unlikely, there is a very large population that continues to perpetrate this myth. This does raise an interesting question though. What if a Grand Master were to posthumously declare a man a Mason at sight? For starters, based on the official process of making a Mason at sight, this would be impossible, as a dead man cannot go through degree work. In the highly hypothetical and unlikely situation that a Grand Master just decided to declare a man a Mason after death without the ceremony what could happen? This is where the "cross Jurisdiction recognition" comes in.

Each Grand Jurisdiction is subject to no one but their own Grand Master in that Jurisdiction. If any Grand Master in any Jurisdiction were to declare a man a Mason posthumously it would not be subject to the debate of any other authority but its own. While this may cause massive ripples in the harmony of the order among other Jurisdiction, the fact is, no other Jurisdiction could stop it from happening. This sort of action would no doubt cause serious recognition repercussions from other Grand Jurisdictions.

Because many other Grand Jurisdictions carry mutual recognition, a Mason made at sight in one state would stand to be a Mason in another as long as each Grand Jurisdiction recognized each other. In that line of thought, any other Grand Jurisdiction that shares recognition with the Jurisdiction in question would also recognize the dead man as a brother.

In Pennsylvania there is limited (although expanding) Prince Hall recognition. If King or any other man were made a Mason posthumously by the Prince Hall Grand Lodge of Georgia it still would not mean all men would recognize him as a brother. In fact, at the current time Prince Hall Masons of Georgia are not recognized by the Pennsylvania Grand Lodge, and so, all so-called "regular" members in Lodges across Pennsylvania would be subject to the Jurisdiction of the Grand Lodge of Pennsylvania and would not recognize Dr. King as a Freemason.

There is no doubt that King carried many outstanding characteristics of a qualified candidate for Freemasonry. In fact his father and Grand Father were both Prince Hall Masons. To put this myth to bed though, King was never made a Freemason. [16]

To sum it all up; it is safe to say that the act of "Making a Mason at Sight" is justified, regulated, and rightfully preformed. The candidates are still given degrees, and the lessons are being told to each person, individually. The Grand Masters who chose to perform this act are neither breaking any landmark nor bending any law of Freemasonry. This is a practice that has been documented for well over 200 years and has not brought about the absolute destruction of the Craft. Hopefully, with a little education, this practice can lose the negative stigma that it has carried for many years. We all can have an opinion on the matter. While it may be justified to disagree with the practice, it is not justified to accuse any Grand Master of malfeasance.

It would wise for us to recognize that no matter how a man is made a Mason, he is only as good of a Mason as he makes himself. Masons at sight and one day class Masons are every bit a member as the next guy. These men have every opportunity, right, and privilege that their Lodges offer every member. To degrade their character or membership based on ignorance of Masonic law or differing opinion on the manner in which they were made a Mason would be truly un-Masonic. We are a brotherhood. We are all with our own strengths and weaknesses.

Mason at Sight Bibliography

1. Pennsylvania Freemason Magazine, Volume LVIII, May 2011, Number 2, page 15.

2. Pennsylvania Freemason Magazine, Volume XLV, November 1998, Number 4

3. Pennsylvania Freemason Magazine, Volume XLIX, February 2002, Number 1

4. Pennsylvania Freemason Magazine, August 1987

5. National Heritage Museum, Making a Mason at Sight, the Case of President-elect Taft. http://nationalheritagemuseum.typepad.com/library_and_archives/william-h-taft/

6. The Grand Lodge of Pennsylvania, newly Made Masons at Site, 2001. http://www.pagrandlodge.org/events/masonsatsite2001/index.html

7. Pennsylvania Freemason Magazine, August 1987

8. Making a Mason at Sight, Bro. Wildey E. Atchison, Colorado, *The Builder,* February 1916 http://www.masonicdictionary.com/sight.html

9. Pennsylvania Freemason Magazine, August 1987

10. Ahiman Rezon; 19.04

11. Ahiman Rezon; 12.03

12. An Encyclopedia of Freemasonry and its Kindred Sciences, Moss and Co., 1874, page 441.

13. The American Tyler-Keystone, decoted to Freemasonry and Its Concerdant Other, Volume 24, Page 55, Craft Movement in Michigan.

14. Proceedings of the Grand Lodge of Ancient, Free, & Accepted Masons of Canada, 1896, page XXXVII

15. Renaissance as to Grand Lodge, PA Freemason Magazine, January 2010, page 15, (Opening and Closing Meetings)

16. http://www.pagrandlodge.org/freemason/0110/page15.html

17. The Texas Prince Hall Freemason, Winter 2001, Page 59-62, Was MLK Jr. a Mason?

Should I look into Appendant and Concordant Bodies?

For many people, after their initial degree work, the first Masonic experience they have is that of having a petition shoved at them from someone asking them to join another body of Freemasonry.

Every Mason will make the decision at some point to get involved in other bodies.   It is important to understand them before jumping in though.

A good practice would be to research them. Find out what the official purpose of these organizations is to be rather than just finding out what title is conferred upon you.

One thing I have learned to do is look at the negatives first. By this, I mean, I look at things like; what good does 5 different sets of dues do if you can never attend the meetings? How active are they?   The overall organization may have a great mission statement and philanthropy, but if it's hard to find out what they actually do, then perhaps you may want to ask around a bit before signing up. Likewise, maybe they are very active and ask all their members to be the same.   If you know you cannot commit to the order the way they expect then you may be doing them a favor by not joining at the current time.

Our fraternity has so many baby fraternities dependent on it that many times it is hard for the new members to make heads or tails of what is Freemasonry and what is simply an organization dependent on Freemasonry.

In a perfect world the candidate would join the Lodge, learn a bit, take it all in, then form an opinion about where they want to move, if anywhere, in Freemasonry. These other bodies of Freemasonry were all born out of the principles learned in Freemasonry, but where you could implement them for use in a specific way. Such is not the case anymore.

We now have so many separate fraternities that claim Masonic connections and require Masonic membership but at the same time do not give the Masonic fraternity the time of day to understand why exactly they do it.

Since there exists next to no rules or regulations requiring clear understandings of Masonic principles before joining many other bodies, and the regulations that currently exist are being relaxed and modified all the time, it is left to the members to police and guide new members on their journey. Again, this is where the ball is dropped many times.

Also, be aware that the Masonic trees and Masonic "family" charts that you see in books are not always as they seem. The highest degree in Freemasonry is the third degree. All other degrees are just that, "other" degrees. They are not "higher" degrees.

In modern Freemasonry these charts can be deceptive as well because they do not always depict the reality of the progression.

A lot has changed in Freemasonry in the past 100 years. It seems a lot of that change has happened in the last 10 years. Our fraternity, which is extremely similar from Jurisdiction to Jurisdiction, also has an endless list of differences that sometimes are confusing to the new Mason.

I will start off with saying that this chapter for both the new Mason looking for more information on other bodies as well as the guy who has maybe made a few missteps by jumping into an appendant or concordant body too quickly. I've put together this chart to illustrate some of these differences as seen by a Pennsylvania Freemason. Much of this can be applied to other Jurisdictions, but being from Pennsylvania, this is how I see it. This is meant to be satire, and maybe even slight criticism of the system, but all in good fun.

As mentioned above, most of us are familiar with the charts that pop up in Masonic books or in the front of your bibles that illustrate the supposed hierarchy of Freemasonry. As a Freemason with a little experience, you should know much of this hierarchical illustration is not as it seems in the pretty charts. By that, I mean, yes, there is a progression; some degrees have prerequisites, and some appear to be the top or pinnacle of Freemasonry. The traditional chart illustration, no doubt, leaves the new Mason feeling like his puny three degrees are worthless. However, after a few years of learning the system, one realizes that that nicely organized chart is misleading. I have created this chart, which is not as pretty, and possibly even just as confusing, to illustrate how I see it.

Another thing about my chart: I've left off the many other appendant bodies of Freemasonry such as AMD, Eastern Star, the youth groups, etc. Here I am focusing on the more common bodies of the York Rite, Scottish Rite, and Shrine.

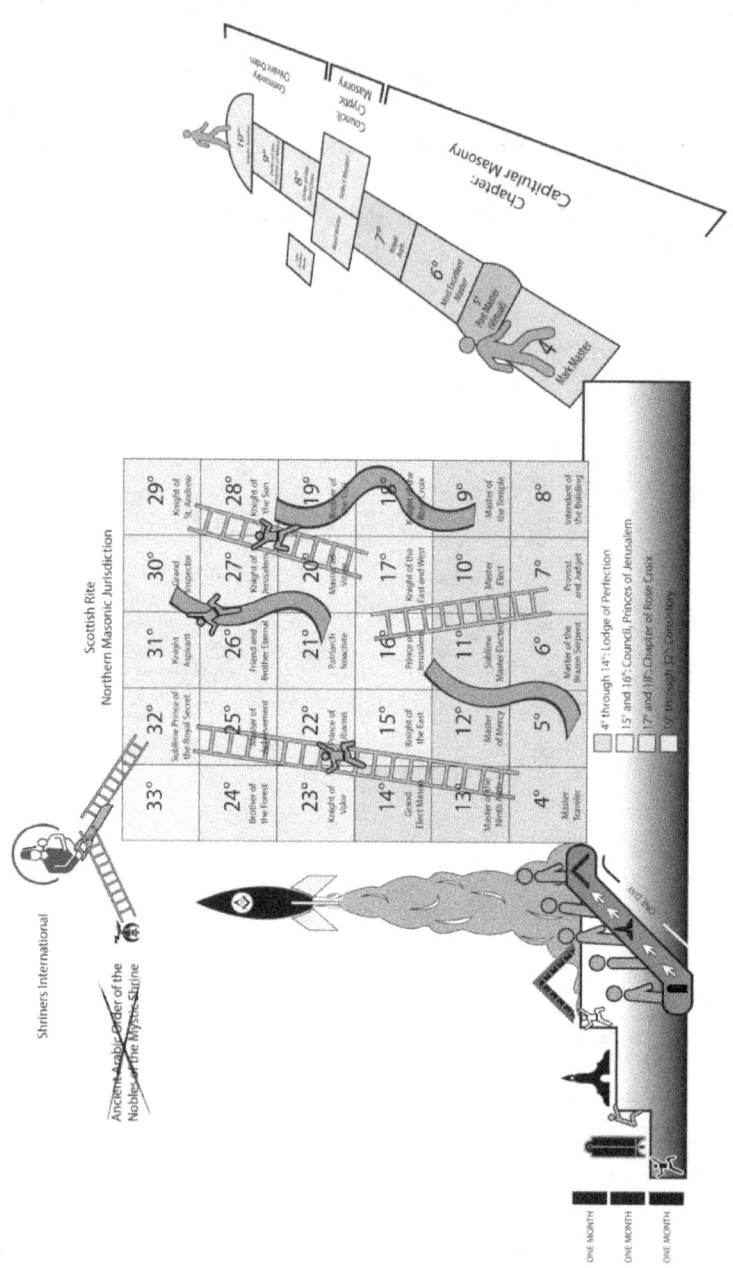

138

Blue Lodge

Looking at this chart you will see that we start much like the common illustrations start, with the first three degrees. A man moves from an entered Apprentice, to Fellow Craft, to Master Mason with the first three degrees in the first three steps. These steps typically take about one month per degree to complete. What is different about my chart, however, is that directly beside the first three steps in Freemasonry is an escalator that takes a man from ground level to Master Mason with no effort and in literally a fraction of the time. In my opinion, the journey from darkness to Masonic light does not happen as it should with the escalator and typically requires a little more work on the candidate to figure out.

The Shrine

From the platform of Master Mason, if one chooses to do so, he can jump directly onto the rocket ship that takes him to Shrine membership. Of course, you'll also see that they become members of Shriners International, not the Ancient Arabic Order of the Nobles of the Mystic Shrine, which no longer exists. Once the new member becomes a Shriner (sometimes a few hours after he becomes a dues paying Mason with a card in his wallet) it takes some time to learn that this new fraternity he is in, which at one time appears at the pinnacle of some Masonic family illustrations, is in fact, no more than separate, but noble, fraternity with very little Masonic connection at all. Even the original logo is falling away as the new logo of Shriners International is slowly cutting the last remaining connection to the Freemasons. This brings us to the next item to cover:

The Scottish Rite

Now, since I am part of the Northern Masonic Jurisdiction of the Scottish Rite, this chart only displays how things are in my neck of the woods. Notice that instead of a clean cut hierarchy of degrees, what we have here is more like the game Chutes and Ladders. The new Mason who just put a Blue Lodge card in his wallet now enters yet even another body of Freemasonry and takes the ladder directly to that glorious number 32 just as immediate as he took the escalator from 1-3. The new member is quickly impressed with everything thrown his way, and is told that he should, at some point in his life, go through and witness all of the degrees of the Scottish rite. The chutes and ladders make this possible. Sometimes the 14th degree is being put on, the next time the 10th and 25th may be put on. Feel free to climb around and slide down back and forth between degrees. What is difficult to illustrate here is that degrees are not always conferred in your local Valley. While each Valley does have the capability to do each degree, the reality is, many do not have a consistent rotation of all of the degrees. If you want all the degrees you will need to hit the road, sometimes traveling across several states to "collect them all." Oh, another thing that is difficult to illustrate is that just because you may have witnessed them all, in the Northern Jurisdiction, they can change from time to time. With this, even if you have seen them all, you may need to see them all again if you want to stay 100% current. This brings us to:

The York Rite

Now, this is yet again confusing to the new Mason who jumps right in. In Pennsylvania at least, our York Rite System differs from many other York Rite Jurisdictions in that we have a Grand Chapter of Pennsylvania. Yep, we have a sovereign and independent Grand Chapter that we share mutual recognition with the some other sovereign state Grand Chapters and the General Grand Chapter International.

In our Grand Chapter there are a series of degrees that run from 4-7. That SHOULD be 4 degrees, although the candidate goes from 4-6, skipping over the 5th degree, or Past Master degree. This gave me the idea to illustrate this entire Rite as game of hopscotch.

In Chapter, new candidates just become what has been dubbed a "Virtual Past Master" when they go from degree 4 to 6. In Pennsylvania, the Past Master degree is actually conferred on you upon being elected to the position of Worshipful Master of your Blue Lodge, and is conferred by the Past Masters of your Lodge. This is where you get the word of the chair and become a Past Master.

Again, this is Pennsylvania, most other Grand Chapters actually have the Past Master degree that give you the word of the chair making you a Past Master, even if you have never served as Master of your Lodge. To complicate it a little more, in most European Lodges there is not a Past Master degree, but an "Install Master" degree. It would be time consuming and monotonous to list all of the differences of individual Jurisdictions in regards to their Past Master degree, but if you want more info a simple internet search for "Past Master Degree" can yield many results.

As the York Rite moves from Chapter, we go into Council, which from there moves on to Commandary. Notice the graphic: the hopscotch graphic gets further away as you move higher up the Rite. I did this to illustrate that in my opinion, as you move further away from Chapter, you get further away from Freemasonry.

While Council still follows closely the story we are familiar with in Blue Lodge dealing with the temple and Hiram Abiff, the degrees deal more with the building/destruction/rebuilding of the temple. It can be confusing to some as it is considered a prerequisite for Commandary in some Jurisdictions, (not in

Pennsylvania) and is a series of three degrees, but only two are required for advancement in York rite, and one is only sometimes put on. This optional, or honorable, degree, Super Excellent Master, is illustrated to the side as it is not always part of the game, and many people chose not to even see it even if offered because they are only doing Council to get to Commandary and the Knight Templar Degree. It is worth repeating here that in some York Rite Jurisdictions Council is not required to go onto Commandary, while in others it is.

From Council we go into Commandary, which is a series of degrees also referred to as the Chivalric Orders by some. These degrees are beautiful, and when correctly put on are said to be some of the most powerful of the entire degree system. As stated above, these degrees are wonderful, but move away from Masonic principles, and some could argue are even un-Masonic altogether. The order of the Knight Templar is conferred upon those only who promise to defend the Christian religion. While this is wonderful for an individual Christian, it is very exclusionary, and goes against one of the most basic tenants of Freemasonry as being "on the level." For guys like me, this is

144

extremely conflicting as I recognize its exclusionary practice, but someday I would like to experience this degree and become a Knight Templar.

So, should you jump directly into another body? I can't tell you one way or another, but it is important to have at least a basic understanding of what these organizations are and what they do. If all you are after is a title, then you really aren't helping any organization you'd become involved in.

What's in it for Me?

You are here because you had a desire to become a Freemason. While you may have been misguided or mislead prior to taking your obligation, hopefully by this point you know exactly what Freemasonry is and is not.

A few missteps do not necessarily make you a failed Mason by any means, but course correction is a MUST if you truly want to gain the benefits of Freemasonry.

With that said, the question is, "What are the benefits of Freemasonry?" In short the answer is a better life, but is that all? Lots of things can create a better life for you. You need not be a Freemason to find better things in your life.

The reality is, just because you have taken the obligations and entered the ranks of Freemasonry does not mean you will get any benefit at all out of the deal.

While there are countless stories of brothers helping brothers, Lodges coming to the side of members down on their luck, fantastic networking and the occasional leg up, you shouldn't count on these being automatic. These are great things, but hardly what should be considered normal benefits of Freemasonry. In fact, many of these would be automatic disqualifiers for your membership if it was known that is what you were after.

We get out of Freemasonry what we put into it. If you purchase a card for your wallet (your dues) every year, but do nothing else, then odds are you will get just that, a card in your wallet, and nothing else.

The more you educate yourself and become involved, not just in the Lodge, but in your daily life, you will see the beauty of the Craft working. However, being an educated Mason does not necessarily mean anything if the Masons you meet along the way are uninformed. Remember, there are many Masons who do not attend meetings or do anything with their membership out there, so odds are when you do meet a Mason, it may not mean a whole lot.

We are a family, and as such it is your duty to constantly stand upright and spread the light of Freemasonry with brotherly love and affection.

Sometimes the personal benefit in your life comes from the fact that you have helped someone personally benefit. Much like gift-giving, it's not about what you receive it's about what you give.

Relief and help can be an enormous benefit from joining any society. Freemasonry may offer that to you, but more importantly it opens you up to being a more charitable person in offering your services to others. I look at charity and relief as more of a "what goes around comes around" system. If I give what I can, I feel it will be noticed when and if I ever need it. If I give nothing, I have no right to expect anyone to offer aid or assistance in my time of need.

Acceptance and tolerance are some of the cornerstones of Freemasonry. While using the working tool of the level we are placed in the same playing field with every single Lodge member. Those who want to grow and produce have the state to do so. Those who do not, will not. Freemasonry is color blind. Freemasonry cares not about your social standing. Freemasonry refines any member who wants to be refined. Our system exists because it works. It works only if we have men using it as it was intended. Opening your heart to those who may otherwise be outside of your comfort zone will open doors to many other worlds you may not typically find yourself in.

What then, makes you a Freemason? Is it paying your dues? Many men think so. Does perfect attendance make you a Freemason? Many men think this as well. Does volunteering, fundraising, or memorizing the ritual make you a Freemason? Again, many men think so.

These are all noble characteristics of a great Mason. The fraternity absolutely needs men to do all the above and more. Why then, question whether any of this stuff makes a man a Freemason?

The answer is because many in our ranks seem to have lost the concept of what it means to be in the Freemasons, and what it means to be a Freemason. Think about this for a moment. Does perfect attendance mean anything if you are not living by the working tools? If you pay your yearly dues, but have no idea what the working tools are, can you truly call yourself a Freemason?

While "the Freemasons" as a whole can be considered a club by some, Freemasonry definitely is not. Freemasonry is much more. Freemasonry is a system of living. Freemasonry is a living system. It's true. Freemasonry, when practiced correctly, is a system of life that teaches self-improvement. A Freemason is supposed to practice Masonic virtues. A Freemason is taught to make use of the working tools of the Craft as symbols to aid and improve their daily lives.

Freemasonry benefits you by turning you into a better man. You are here because you were a decent man to begin with. Freemasonry elevates you to the next level.

While it is easy to understand this, we can also look at the other aspects and benefits of Freemasonry. While in many aspects Freemasonry is about making your life better, another side effect of it is that it also prepares you to die.

We are on this Earth for a very short period of time. As a Freemason in a regularly recognized Lodge you, like all regular Freemasons have a belief in a Supreme Being. Is it not all of our goals at the end of this life to walk through the gates of Heaven and live eternal in peace?

When we move from this earthly world to become a block of that spiritual temple in the heavens we want to be as close to perfect as possible. While your faith and religion can teach you salvation, Freemasonry can guide your actions to help you in your journey. While not being a religion, Freemasonry is certainly a sidekick to religion; making you a more charitable, giving, helpful, thoughtful and well-rounded citizen.

Conclusion

A lot can be said about the Masonic fraternity. It's a large monster. There are so many different aspects of the fraternity that a man could literally read a new book every day for the rest of his life trying to understand it and still not be an expert on all things Masonic. Being that there are so many faces of Freemasonry, it can sometimes be difficult to explain any one particular avenue of the Craft without at least touching on the many other facets of the fraternity. One could break down Masonry into categories of history, tradition, morals, practices, ritual, or knowledge to try and cover all the basic aspects of the Craft and there would still be more to talk about. Along with such a large and complicated organization comes a plethora of men making the wheels turn. These men come from all different backgrounds and professions. These men all have their own strengths and weaknesses. Every man in the fraternity can bring something to the good of the group if he chooses. Likewise, it's important for even the most organized of men to understand that any man who tries to run everything himself can cause ripples in the harmony of the order. It is important for us to all participate where we can and at the same time also invite and include others. While our system isn't perfect, it is our system and it is up to us to use it to its fullest.

The purpose of Freemasonry is to make a good man a better man. While I have a vision of how Freemasonry should work, it is just that, MY

VISION. There may be another guy who becomes a better person out there while taking all the shortcuts available to him. In that case, Freemasonry worked for that guy too. It is possible to disagree with everything I have written in this book and still be getting a sense of self betterment out of the fraternity.

We are all brothers, we are all human. My hope is that my opinion can help others view the system in a slightly different manner. Maybe it will be an eye opener; maybe it will make some folks mad. The point is, you can use Freemasonry to its fullest, or you can use parts of it as it fits your life. Educate yourself, and then try to educate others.

Being a Freemason cannot be accomplished through any amount of memorization, volunteering, charity, or good deeds. All of the above will certainly make you a great person, and a true Freemason should have all of the above qualities, but these items cannot on their own make you a Freemason. After all, a person outside our fraternity can volunteer, give to charity, do nothing but good deeds, and if he somehow stumbles upon our ritual, could also memorize the entire thing.

Let's assume for a moment that a man, outside our West Gate, was to do all of the above. Does that make him a Mason? If you have any other thought in your head other than a very loud and clear NO, then perhaps it is time for some basic Masonic education.

What then, makes the Masons stand out? Why are they any different than the Moose or the Elks or the Rotary? Why does one need to join the Masons to do charitable things? The short answer is you don't. If you wanted to do charitable things, then any of these great organizations will be able to fulfill your desire to do so.

Perhaps if all you want to do is volunteer and do charity, then maybe the Masons are not a great fit for you. Not because you are not a good person, but because that is not what Freemasonry is solely about.

To put it in other words, the great list of positive things the Masons can lay claim to are not necessarily a result of us being a so called civic club. On the contrary, one could argue that the "club" many see is a side effect of the members just practicing Masonic virtues.

Here lies the problem. In today's world, unfortunately, many Masons cannot tell you why we are different from other fraternal organizations. Some men will sit on the sidelines for years and complain about "never doing anything." They will follow with comparisons of other civil organizations who are doing overwhelmingly well in attendance and charity and ask why we do not do these things. Others will avoid meetings because they are "boring." There is always a reason to find fault in any organization, but for some reason in Freemasonry we have an overwhelming number of men who have no clue what Freemasonry is about, but yet insist we should be "out there" doing things.

This may be difficult for some to listen to, but as stated above, those who truly live by Masonic virtues and make use of the working tools in their daily lives will, by default, not only see the great benefits of Freemasonry, but will also gain an understanding of what Freemasonry is. They will understand why just "being in the Freemasons" is not enough to actually BE a Freemason. You have to go out and earn it!